Shaping IASC for the Future

**A Discussion Paper issued for comment by the
Strategy Working Party
of the International Accounting Standards Committee**

Comments to be submitted by 30 April 1999

This Discussion Paper is issued by the Strategy Working Party of the International Accounting Standards Committee for comment only. The Discussion Paper has not been considered by the Board of the International Accounting Standards Committee and does not necessarily represent the views of the Board.

Comments should be submitted in writing so as to be received by **30 April 1999**. All replies will be placed on the public record unless confidentiality is requested by the commentator. If commentators respond by fax or E-mail, it would be helpful if they could also send a hard copy of their response by post. Comments should be addressed to:

The Secretary-General
International Accounting Standards Committee
166 Fleet Street
London EC4A 2DY
United Kingdom

Fax: +44 (0171) 353-0562
E-mail: CommentLetters@iasc.org.uk

Executive Summary and Invitation to Comment

The International Accounting Standards Committee (IASC) completed the last review of its strategy and structure in 1994. Since then, IASC's main focus has been on a work programme, agreed with the International Organization of Securities Commissions (IOSCO), to complete a set of core standards that would be suitable for cross-border capital raising and listing purposes in all global markets. IASC plans to finish the work programme in 1998.

The completion of the core standards programme agreed with IOSCO is now imminent. However, challenging work still lies ahead for IASC. In particular, IASC needs to bring about convergence between national accounting standards and practices and high-quality global accounting standards. To this end, IASC needs an effective infrastructure that will bring its experience and current work together with those of national standard setters. Therefore, the IASC Board formed a Strategy Working Party in 1997 to consider what IASC's strategy and structure should be when it completes the work programme. The Strategy Working Party's terms of reference and membership are set out in Appendix 2.

The Strategy Working Party has approved this Discussion Paper to stimulate and focus discussion. The Working Party will consider the comments received on this Discussion Paper before preparing a final report to the IASC Board. In the meantime, members of the Working Party will be pleased to discuss the Discussion Paper with commentators.

A summary of the Working Party's recommendations is set out below. Following this summary, the Working Party has set out a number of questions. The Working Party welcomes answers to these questions and comments on any other aspects of the Discussion Paper. Comments should be submitted in writing so as to be received by **30 April 1999**.

EXECUTIVE SUMMARY

Introduction

1. International Accounting Standards have done a great deal both to improve and to harmonise financial reporting around the world. They are used:

    (a)   as a basis for national accounting requirements in many countries;

    (b)   as an international benchmark by some countries that develop their own requirements (including certain major industrialised countries, regional organisations such as the European Union, and an increasing number of emerging markets such as China and many other countries in Asia, Central Europe and the countries of the former Soviet Union);

    (c)   by stock exchanges and regulatory authorities that allow foreign or domestic companies to present financial statements in accordance with International Accounting Standards;

    (d)   by supra-national bodies that rely on IASC to produce accounting standards that improve the quality of financial reporting and the comparability of financial statements, instead of developing their own requirements;

(e)   by the World Bank Group and other development agencies that require borrowers and recipients of other forms of aid to follow high standards of financial reporting and accountability; and

(f)   by a growing number of individual companies.

2.   IASC has been successful in developing high quality International Accounting Standards that have gained increasing acceptance around the world. To build on that achievement, the Working Party believes that IASC should now be anticipating future needs and modifying its own role and structure in response to major changes in the environment in which IASC operates. Although IASC's existing structure has served it well, the Working Party believes that IASC needs to change its structure so that it can meet new challenges, and seize new opportunities, as effectively as it has met other challenges in the first 25 years of its life.

3.   In recent years, changes in IASC's environment have placed strain on the organisational and financial resources of a body that relies, as IASC does, extensively on work by volunteers and on relatively informal contacts with national standard setters. The most important of these changes are:

(a)   a rapid growth in international capital markets, combined with an increase in cross-border listings and cross-border investment. These have led to efforts by securities regulators to develop a common "passport" for cross-border securities listings and to achieve greater comparability in financial reporting;

(b)   efforts of global organisations (such as the World Trade Organisation) and regional bodies (such as the European Union, NAFTA, MERCOSUR and APEC) to dismantle barriers to international world trade;

(c)   a trend towards the internationalisation of business regulation;

(d)   increasing influence of International Accounting Standards on national accounting requirements and practice;

(e)   accelerating innovation in business transactions;

(f)   increasing demand from users for new types of financial and other performance information;

(g)   new developments in the electronic distribution of financial and other performance information; and

(h)   growing need for relevant and reliable financial and other performance information both in countries in transition from planned economies to market economies and in developing and newly industrialised economies.

4.   These trends show a clear and growing demand from the market for the world to have high-quality global accounting standards that provide transparency and comparability. Indeed in October 1998:

(a)   the G-22 Working Party on Transparency and Accountability reported that: "weaknesses in the provision and use of information played a major part in the development and spread of recent international financial crises." The report called for "a set of high quality, internationally acceptable accounting standards"; and

(b)   a declaration of G7 Finance Ministers and Central Bank Governors on 30 October stated, among other things: "We call upon (...) the IASC to finalise by early 1999 a proposal for a full range of internationally agreed accounting standards. IOSCO, IAIS, and the Basle Committee should complete a timely review of these standards. (...) We commit ourselves to endeavour to ensure that private sector institutions in our countries comply with these principles, standards and codes of best practice. We call upon (...) all countries which participate in global capital markets similarly to commit to comply with these internationally agreed codes and standards (...)"

Similarly, the Chairman of the Basle Committee on Banking Supervision has stated that "the Basle Committee considers transparency to be a key element of an effectively supervised, safe and sound banking system".

5.   IASC's international structure and record of success have put it in a unique position to satisfy the demand for high-quality global accounting standards. However, IASC cannot take further success for granted. Among other things:

(a)   IASC's role in the future is unlikely to be the same as in the past. In its early years, IASC acted mainly as a harmoniser - a body that selects an accounting treatment that already exists at the national level in some countries and then seeks worldwide acceptance of that treatment, perhaps with some modifications. IASC's current structure has enabled IASC to play an effective role as a harmoniser. In more recent times, it has begun to combine that role with the role of a catalyst - a co-ordinator of national initiatives and an initiator of new work at the national level. In the future, IASC's role as a catalyst and initiator should become more prominent;

(b)   the significance of IASC's work has increased vastly in recent years. IASC's structure worked well when IASC's work affected a relatively small number of countries and enterprises. There is no guarantee that this structure will work without modification at a time when IASC's work has a direct or indirect effect in almost every country;

(c)   innovation in business transactions is accelerating, demand from users for new types of financial and other performance information is increasing and there are rapid developments in electronic distribution of information. Also, the life cycle of standards in all fields – not just in accounting – is shrinking rapidly. In recent years, IASC has taken on a more innovatory role in certain areas, such as financial instruments. The Working Party believes that in future IASC will need to be an innovator and an initiator to a much greater extent than it is today. IASC needs a structure that will enable it to cope effectively with these and other new developments; and

(d)   since the beginning of 1997, IASC has been able to increase the length and frequency of Board meetings for the specific objective of completing the core standards programme agreed with IOSCO. It would be difficult for a group of volunteers to sustain this level of activity indefinitely.

6.   An increasingly important challenge for IASC will be to work with national standard setters to bring about convergence between national accounting standards and International Accounting Standards around solutions requiring listed enterprises (i.e. enterprises with publicly traded equity or debt securities) and other economically significant enterprises to report high-quality, transparent and comparable information that will help participants in capital markets and others to make economic decisions. The standards of many countries are already converging with International Accounting Standards. However, trends such as globalisation and the increasing pace of business and financial change have made this task more urgent. The Working Party believes that IASC and national standard setters need to find new ways of working together to minimise unnecessary delays in reaching consensus and implementing the results of that consensus.

7.   In the Working Party's view, IASC must now consider structural changes so that it can continue to meet the need for high-quality global accounting standards. If IASC fails to meet that need, other national, regional or international bodies are likely to emerge to fill the gap in response to market pressures and become de facto global or regional standard setters.

Objectives of IASC

8.   The objectives of IASC as stated in its Constitution are:

(a)   to formulate and publish in the public interest accounting standards to be observed in the presentation of financial statements and to promote their worldwide acceptance and observance; and

(b)   to work generally for the improvement and harmonisation of regulations, accounting standards and procedures relating to the presentation of financial statements.

9.   In the Working Party's view, it is important to focus IASC's objectives more precisely as follows:

(a)   to develop International Accounting Standards that require high-quality, transparent and comparable information which will help participants in capital markets and others to make economic decisions; and

(b)   to promote the use of International Accounting Standards by working with national standard setters to:

(i)   bring about convergence, for listed enterprises (i.e. enterprises with publicly traded equity or debt securities) and other economically significant enterprises, between national accounting standards and International Accounting Standards; and

(ii)   encourage national, regional and international authorities to permit or require unlisted enterprises that, individually, are not economically significant to use those International Accounting Standards if those Standards meet the needs of the users of the financial statements of such enterprises.

10. The Working Party believes that it is vital for IASC to continue to use an agreed conceptual Framework (the Framework for the Preparation and Presentation of Financial Statements) to ensure that its standards are of high quality and require transparent and comparable information to help participants in capital markets and others to make economic decisions. The Framework may need to be revised from time to time on the basis of IASC's experience of working with it.

11. The Working Party strongly supports the Framework's focus on information that will meet the needs of the capital markets and so also meet most of the common needs of other users.

12. The Working Party believes that IASC should continue, in close partnership with national standard setters and other constituents, to play an innovatory role in areas of increasing importance to IASC's constituents. Such areas may include:

   (a) the growing use of new technology, such as the Internet and CD-ROMs, to deliver financial information in new ways. This may create a need for different or additional types of financial reporting standards; and

   (b) emerging issues such as environmental reporting and accounting for human resources and intellectual capital;

   (c) broader aspects of financial and other performance reporting outside the traditional financial statements, for example:

      (i) financial reporting in a Management Discussion and Analysis ('MD&A'), Directors' Report, or similar document; and

      (ii) prospective financial information; and

      (iii) non-financial measures of performance.

13. The Working Party believes that IASC should, in developing International Accounting Standards, and in promoting their use, work closely with national standard setters to reach mutual agreement on what the highest quality result is. The aim is to ensure that national accounting standards and International Accounting Standards converge around high-quality solutions. The Working Party believes that IASC should work for convergence by:

   (a) continuing to develop International Accounting Standards that build on the best features of existing and newly developed national standards. For topics where national standards do not yet exist, or are still evolving, IASC will need to work with national standard setters to develop high-quality requirements that lead to transparency and comparability;

   (b) acting as a catalyst for, or initiator of, national developments in standard setting; and

   (c) keeping existing International Accounting Standards under review in the light of the latest thinking at national and international levels. In some cases, this review may lead to the conclusion that a national standard provides greater transparency or comparability than an existing International Accounting

Standard. In such cases, IASC will need to consider amending its existing Standard.

14. The Working Party believes that IASC should, in partnership with national standard setters, make every effort to accelerate convergence between national and International Accounting Standards around solutions requiring listed and other economically significant enterprises in all countries to report high-quality, transparent and comparable information that will help participants in capital markets and others to make economic decisions. Although IASC and national standard setters have worked together successfully and narrowed the differences between accounting standards and procedures in different countries, the remaining differences cannot be eliminated overnight. In the Working Party's view:

(a) IASC's short-term aim should be for national accounting standards and International Accounting Standards to converge around high-quality solutions; and

(b) IASC's aim in the longer term should be global uniformity - a single set of high-quality accounting standards for all listed and other economically significant business enterprises around the world. It is not possible to forecast how long this will take, as different countries are likely to converge with uniform global standards at different rates.

15. The Working Party believes that:

(a) regulators and standard setters in each country should decide, in the light of local circumstances:

(i) whether International Accounting Standards are appropriate for small and medium-sized enterprises (SMEs) in that country;

(ii) how SMEs should be defined in that country; and

(iii) what accounting standards should be used by SMEs in that country; and

(b) it is likely that many countries will choose to bring accounting standards for smaller enterprises into line with International Accounting Standards. Therefore, IASC must be prepared to re-evaluate the entire package of International Accounting Standards from the view point of smaller enterprises.

16. In April 1998, the IASC Board approved a proposal for a project to investigate the accounting needs of countries in transition to a market economy and developing and newly industrialised countries. The Working Party supports IASC's continuing investigations in this area.

17. IASC's Constitution does not limit IASC's objectives to financial reporting by business enterprises. The Working Party believes that:

    (a) IASC should continue to concentrate on business enterprises in the private sector for the time being and maintain a close dialogue with the Public Sector Committee of IFAC, the International Federation of Accountants; and

    (b) IASC should not focus on financial reporting by not-for-profit organisations, such as charities, at this stage. However, it is likely to become important for IASC to address this topic at some point in the future.

Structure of IASC

18. The current structure of IASC has significant strengths:

    (a) IASC has produced high-quality standards that command international support, without unnecessary delay, generally by using existing national standards as a starting point;

    (b) the geographical spread of Board membership, and the requirement that a final standard must achieve a positive vote from three-quarters of the Board as currently constituted, mean that IASC must persuade a reasonably broad constituency that its proposals are appropriate - an important consideration for an organisation that cannot compel countries or individual enterprises to adopt its standards. At the same time, the required majority is not so high that progress is blocked;

    (c) most Board delegations are currently made up of three individuals (two Board Representatives and one Technical Adviser). This permits a functional mix (preparers, auditors, standard setters, financial analysts, academics and others) from most countries on the Board and gives the Board the broad perspective that comes from a diversity of backgrounds;

    (d) the part-time status of Board Representatives and technical advisers enables them to stay in touch with their constituents and to retain up-to-date experience of accounting practice in their countries;

    (e) continuity of Board membership (both delegations and their individual representatives) speeds progress, promotes consistency and builds an atmosphere of collegiality and trust which is very important;

    (f) the involvement of a wide range of people in IASC's process, through both the Board itself and Steering Committees, plays an important promotional and educational role for IASC; and

    (g) IASC functions at remarkably low direct cost.

19. IASC has achieved a great deal with the current structure. It has developed high-quality and credible standards. Its standards are widely accepted by the international capital markets. A growing number of countries are either adopting International Accounting Standards as their own standards (in some cases, with relatively minor modifications) or drastically reducing provisions in their own standards that conflict with International Accounting Standards.

20.   Despite the strengths of IASC's current structure, the changes in IASC's environment mean that structural changes are needed so that IASC can anticipate the new challenges facing it and meet those challenges effectively. The Working Party has identified the following key issues that must be addressed:

(a)   partnership with national standard setters - IASC should enter into a partnership with national standard setters so that IASC can work together with them to accelerate convergence between national standards and International Accounting Standards around solutions requiring high-quality, transparent and comparable information that will help participants in capital markets and others to make economic decisions;

(b)   wider participation in the IASC Board - a wider group of countries and organisations should take part in the IASC Board, without diluting the quality of the Board's work; and

(c)   appointment - the process for appointments to the IASC Board and key IASC committees should be the responsibility of a variety of constituencies, while ensuring that those appointed are competent, independent and objective.

The Working Party's proposals for making IASC's due process more effective are addressed in a separate section below.

21.   The Working Party's proposals address these key issues by the following changes:

(a)   a partnership with national standard setters:

(i)   Steering Committees would be replaced by a Standards Development Committee, on which national standard setters would play a major role in developing International Accounting Standards. The Standards Development Committee would also be responsible for approving the publication of final SIC Interpretations prepared by the Standing Interpretations Committee; and

(ii)   the Standards Development Committee would be supported by a Standards Development Advisory Committee, which would act as a channel of communication with those national standard setters who are unable to participate directly in the Standards Development Committee because of its limited size;

(b)   wider participation in the IASC Board - the Board would have a wider membership than at present. The Board would still be responsible for the final approval of International Accounting Standards and Exposure Drafts; and

(c)   appointment - the Advisory Council would be replaced by Trustees. Among other things, the Trustees would appoint members of the Standards Development Committee, the Board and the Standing Interpretations Committee. The Trustees would also have responsibility for monitoring IASC's effectiveness and for finance.

10

22. Table 1 summarises the Working Party's proposals in these areas. Table 2 summarises certain consequential changes that the Working Party proposes. Figures 1 and 2 portray the current structure and the proposed new structure as organisation charts.

Table 1 - Summary of Amended Structure for IASC

Trustees	Board	Standards Development Committee (SDC)
Function Appoint Board, SDC and SIC Members and Board, SDC and SIC Chairmen, on recommendation of Selection Sub-Committee. Liaise with Board Members on appointment of Board Delegates. Trustees retain veto over their appointment (veto requires 9 votes out of 12).	Board Members appoint their Board Delegates, in consultation with Trustees.	
Ratify appointment (by SDC Chairman) of Technical Director and Commercial Director. Promote and ensure independence and objectivity of the Board, SDC and SIC. Do not participate in technical decisions or intervene in technical disputes between SDC and the Board.	Approve Exposure Draft or Standard from the SDC. Discuss main technical issues in depth with SDC at an early stage and as projects progress.	Develop Standards and EDs and submit to the Board. May issue Draft Statements of Principles, Discussion Papers and similar documents.
	Regular guidance to SDC on its work plan. May add projects to SDC work plan, but not delete them.	May add projects to work plan or delete them. Consult Standards Development Advisory Committee. May set up task forces etc. or outsource detailed research to national standard setters.
	Comment on final SIC Interpretations before final SDC vote.	Approve final SIC Interpretations
Monitor effectiveness of IASC's structure and of the SDC and Board. Review broad strategic issues and political relationships. Promote IASC and its work.	Advise Trustees on broad strategic issues and political relationships. Explain and promote IASC's work.	Advise Trustees on broad strategic issues and political relationships. Explain and promote IASC's work.

Table 1 (Continued)

Trustees	Board	Standards Development Committee
Fund-raising. Also, approve IASC's budget and monitor efficient use of its resources. Publish an annual written report on IASC's activities and work of the Trustees. Report to members of IASC every two and a half years	No responsibility for fund-raising	No responsibility for fund-raising
Membership 12 Trustees (individuals): • 6 appointed by constituents (3 from IFAC, 3 from bodies such as those currently on the Consultative Group), in consultation with existing Trustees. • 6 'at large', appointed by the Trustees on recommendation of a Selection Sub-Committee. First 6 'at large' Trustees - appointed by Nominating Committee (current Advisory Council plus recent Chairmen of IASC/IFAC). All unpaid, except Chairman (part-time)	25 members (organisations): • 20 country seats for professional accountancy bodies • 5 seats for other organisations with an interest in financial reporting Each delegation represented by two part-time Board Delegates.	11 members (individuals): • Full-time Chairman • 6 to 8 voting members of their national standard setter (with sufficient technical, human and financial resources) • 2 to 4 from other groups (e.g. preparers, users, accountants in public practice, academics and, perhaps, regulators)
	All unpaid, except Chairman (part-time)	Full-time Chairman (effectively the Chief Executive Officer). At least 6 others full time, and all at least half-time (including time at national standard setter).
May appoint Board Observers	Observers (may speak but not vote): • SDC Members • IOSCO • European Commission • IFAC President (and chairs of IFAC's Public Sector and International Auditing Practices Committees) • Others (not many, but no formal limit) who can contribute to discussion	No observers (but meetings open to public) SDC Members cannot be Board Delegates, but others from same country or organisation (other than a standard setter) may.

13

Table 1 (Continued)

Trustees	Board	Standards Development Committee
Factors considered in selection:		
• Integrity, objectivity and commitment to maintain IASC as an organisation that develops high-quality standards. Act in public interest, not sectional interests.	• Board Delegates to have technical competence, commitment to Framework, integrity and objectivity. Act in public interest, not sectional interests.	• Technical competence, commitment to Framework, integrity and objectivity. Act in public interest, not sectional interests.
• Most from more developed countries, but preferably some from developing countries / countries in transition	• At least 14 more developed countries and at least 4 developing countries / countries in transition	• If qualified candidates available, at least 7 from more developed countries and at least two from developing countries/countries in transition
• Geographical and other balance	• Geographical and other balance	• Geographical and other balance
• Special consideration to countries that use IAS or have high proportion of foreign operations / foreign trade	• Special consideration to countries that use IAS or have high proportion of foreign operations / foreign trade	• Special consideration to countries that use IAS or have high proportion of foreign operations / foreign trade
• Able to make an active contribution to the work of the Trustees	• Able to make an active contribution to the work of the Board	• Able to make an active contribution to the work of the SDC
Term Five years (renewable once). Six of first trustees (3 'constituency' and 3 'at large') to retire after two and a half years	Two and a half years, renewable without limit at discretion of the Trustees. No permanent seats. Planned rotation to balance continuity and turnover.	5 years, renewable once at discretion of the Trustees. First terms staggered. May subsequently appoint another individual from the same organisation.
Chairman Part-time non-executive (paid). Appointed by Trustees, on advice of Selection Sub-committee. First Chairman appointed by Nominating Committee (current Advisory Council plus recent past Chairmen of IASC and IFAC)	Part-time (50%) non-executive (paid). Appointed by Trustees. Main ambassador for IASC.	Appointed by Trustees. Full-time, effectively Chief Executive Officer. Some representative duties.

Table 1 (Continued)

Trustees	Board	Standards Development Committee
Voting To veto appointment of a Board Delegate - 75% (9 out of 12).	1 vote per delegation. To approve Standard or ED 60% (15 out of 25). If 9 or more SDC members vote to resubmit a proposal rejected by the Board, Board approval will require a simple majority (13 out of 25).	Submit Standard or ED to the Board - 7 out of 11. Approve final SIC Interpretation - 7 out of 11.
Propose changes to Constitution - 60% (8 out of 12): with approval by the Members of IASC (simple majority of those voting) and Board. Other decisions - simple majority of those present	Approve changes to Constitution - 60% (15 out of 25, as for Standard): also need approval by the Members of IASC and Trustees. Other decisions - simple majority of those present	Other decisions (including issuing DSOP, Discussion Paper etc.) - simple majority of those present
Finance IASC to pay travel on IASC business and IASC staff support.	IASC to pay travel costs for one Board Delegate attending Board meetings. Board members to pay travel costs to Board meetings for second Board Delegate.	National standard setters and other constituencies to pay salaries, related costs, travel between IASC and home base and domestic staff support. IASC may pay for well-qualified individuals from poor countries or constituencies. IASC to pay travel on IASC business and IASC staff support.
Meetings 2-3 times a year. Partly open to the public at the discretion of the Trustees	3 times a year. Open to the public for discussion of technical issues.	Every 1-2 months. Open to the public for discussion of technical issues.

15

Table 2 - Amended Structure for IASC: Other Points

1.   Members of IASC

Membership   As today - professional accountancy bodies that are members of IFAC

Chairman   None - meetings chaired by Chairman of Trustees

Functions   Receive report by Trustees
             Approval needed for changes to the Constitution (simple majority of those
             voting)

Meetings   Every two and a half years

2.   Consultative Group

Membership   As today - organisations (mainly international) with an interest in financial
             reporting that are not voting members of the Board

Chairman   None - meetings chaired by Chairman of Board

Functions   Give feedback on IASC proposals, guidance on work plan priorities and
             advice on political relationships

             Receive reports on IASC's work

Meetings   1-2 times a year

3.   Standing Interpretations Committee

Membership   12 individuals (as today). Observers: One Board Liaison Member; SDC
             Chairman; others as necessary (currently two: IOSCO, European
             Commission). All appointed by the Trustees or a sub-committee of Trustees.

Chairman   Separate Chairman - part-time, unpaid.

Functions   Approve and publish draft Interpretations. Submit final Interpretations to SDC
             for approval.

Meetings   Four times a year

Table 2 (Continued)

4.   **Standards Development Advisory Committee**

Membership   Standard setters of countries not represented on SDC, at the invitation of the Trustees.

Chairman   SDC Chairman

Functions   Advise SDC whether its proposals are likely to be appropriate and operational in the domestic environment of the countries concerned.

Meetings   At least annually

5.   **Staff**

Technical   Technical functions headed by Technical Director, appointed by the SDC Chairman (after ratification by the Trustees) and reporting to the SDC

Commercial   Commercial functions (including funding, copyright, office, equipment, communications) headed by Commercial Director, appointed by the SDC Chairman (after ratification by the Trustees) and reporting through the SDC Chairman to the Trustees.

Figure 1 - IASC – Current Structure

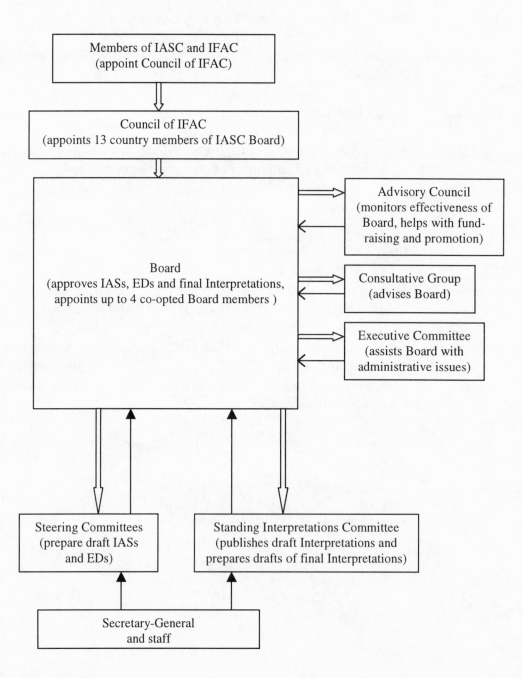

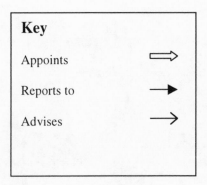

Figure 2 - IASC – Proposed New Structure

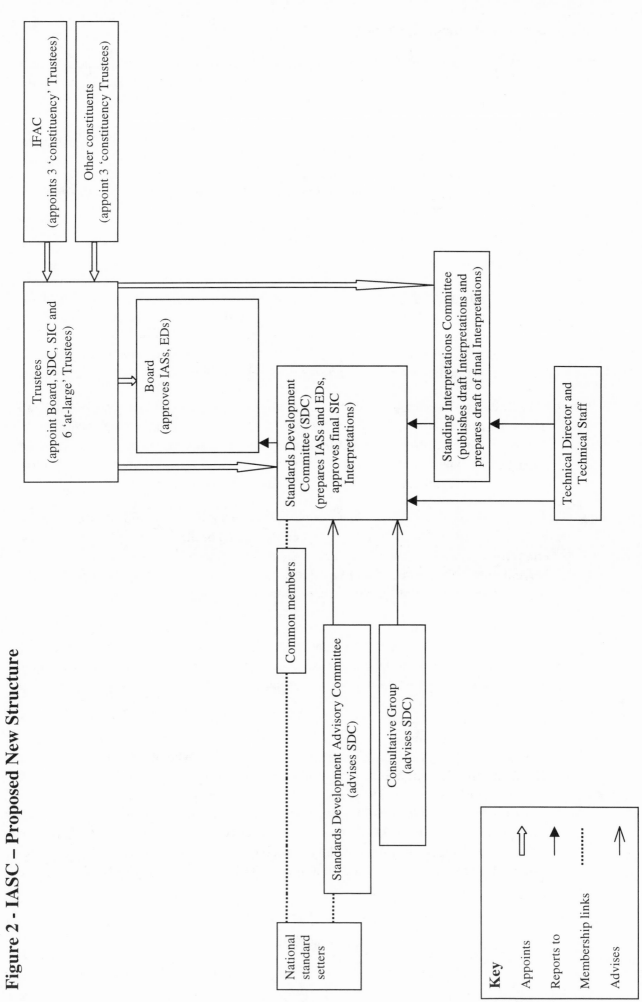

IFAC
(appoints 3 'constituency' Trustees)

Other constituents
(appoint 3 'constituency Trustees)

Trustees
(appoint Board, SDC, SIC and
6 'at-large' Trustees)

Board
(approves IASs, EDs)

**Standards Development
Committee (SDC)**
(prepares IASs and EDs,
approves final SIC
Interpretations)

Standing Interpretations Committee
(publishes draft Interpretations and
prepares draft of final Interpretations)

**Technical Director and
Technical Staff**

Common members

Standards Development Advisory Committee
(advises SDC)

Consultative Group
(advises SDC)

**National
standard
setters**

Key

Appoints

Reports to

Membership links

Advises

19

Approval of International Accounting Standards

23.   The Working Party paid close attention to the question of the final authority to issue standards.   In its discussions, the Working Party identified three crucial considerations:

(a)   the need to convince users, preparers and IASC's other constituents that IASC's standards will meet their needs;

(b)   the need to attract suitably qualified individuals to serve on the Standards Development Committee and the Board; and

(c)   the need for the Standards Development Committee and the Board to work together closely and effectively for the public interest.

24.   IASC cannot force anyone to use its Standards and so must rely on persuasion. It can persuade its constituents to use its Standards only if the Standards are of high quality and meet their needs.   Also, IASC's constituents are more likely to use its Standards if they have a stake in, and play a part in, their development and participation by IASC's constituents is likely to improve the quality of the Standards.

25.   One way to persuade IASC's constituents to accept its due process and its standards would be to set up an autonomous body of independent full-time and highly skilled experts, with a relatively small number of members for the sake of efficiency (an independent expert model).   Another route would be to create a more broadly-based group from a larger number of countries and backgrounds (a constituency model).

26.   The Working Party believes that neither of these extremes would secure sufficient worldwide support from IASC's constituents. Instead, the Working Party's proposal combines elements of both models: a group of independent experts (the Standards Development Committee) and a broader group (the Board), coupled with a high level of due process to ensure a wide range of input.

27.   In developing its proposals, the Working Party was conscious of the need to attract talented and well-qualified individuals to serve on both the Standards Development Committee and the Board. It is unlikely that such individuals will make themselves available for a body that does not have genuine decision-making power.

28.   It is clear that any structure that involves two bodies with genuine decision-making power can work only if the two bodies demonstrate a clear willingness to work together closely and effectively for the public interest. The Working Party believes that a constructive attitude of close and effective co-operation is a striking feature of the current Board and of IASC's Committees. Consequently, the Working Party is confident that the Standards Development Committee and the Board will achieve the close and effective relationship that will be needed. The Working Party also noted that constructive co-operation will not emerge if either the Standards Development Committee or the Board is unable to attract suitably qualified individuals.

29.   With these three considerations in mind, the Working Party considered a range of different ways of specifying the respective powers of the Standards Development Committee and the Board. Among these were:

(a)   positive approval required by a majority or super-majority of the Board for all International Accounting Standards and Exposure Drafts;

(b)   the Board (or perhaps a specified majority or a specified minority of the Board) has the power to reject proposed International Accounting Standards and Exposure Drafts;

(c)   the Board (or perhaps a specified majority or a specified minority of the Board) has the power to return proposed International Accounting Standards and Exposure Drafts to the Standards Development Committee for re-consideration, but not to reject them indefinitely; and

(d)   the Standards Development Committee must consult the Board, but the Board has no power to delay or reject International Accounting Standards or Exposure Drafts.

30.   Individual members of the Working Party have preferences for different points in this range. Some members of the Working Party prefer option (a) above. Other members of the Working Party prefer option (d) above. However, the Working Party believes that the precise voting arrangements are less important than the need for the Standards Development Committee and the Board to work together constructively. As explained above, the Working Party is confident that the Standards Development Committee and the Board will achieve the close and effective relationship that will be needed.

31.   The Working Party proposes that the publication of a Standard or Exposure Draft should require approval by 60% of the Board (15 votes out of 25). At present, an Exposure Draft requires a positive vote by two thirds of the Board; a final Standard requires a positive vote by three quarters of the Board. The Working Party further concluded that the Chairman of the Board should be required to ensure that the Board considers and votes on all proposed Exposure Drafts and Standards submitted by the Standards Development Committee within three months of receipt or, if later, at its next meeting.

32.   If the Board rejects a proposed Exposure Draft or Standard, the Board should send the document back to the Standards Development Committee for further consideration, giving public reasons for its rejection. After considering the reasons given by the Board, the Standards Development Committee may decide to:

(a)   prepare a revised proposal and submit it to the Board for approval in the normal way; or

(b)   resubmit its original proposal to the Board:

(i)   if nine or more members of the Standards Development Committee have voted to resubmit the same proposal, Board approval should require a simple majority (13 votes out of 25); and

(ii)   if seven or eight members of the Standards Development Committee have voted to resubmit the proposal, the proposal should be treated in the same way as a new proposal. In other words, Board approval should require the normal 60% majority (i.e. 15 votes out of 25).

33.   At present, each delegation has one vote. This means that Board delegations are sometimes forced to abstain where the members of the delegation are unable to agree among themselves. Given the current requirement for a positive vote by three quarters of the Board, an abstention is effectively the same as a vote against a Standard. This might suggest that each member of the delegation should be given an individual vote, to reduce the risk of deadlock. However, discussions among, say, 50 voting individuals would be much more cumbersome than discussions among 50 individuals representing 25 voting delegations. The Working Party recommends that IASC should retain the current practice that each delegation has one vote.

34.   The Working Party believes that the Board should not have the power to amend proposed Exposure Drafts and Standards submitted by the Standards Development Committee.

35.   The Working Party believes that the proposals set out in paragraphs 30 to 33 will ensure reasonably widespread acceptance for IASC's work, without undue risk of paralysing the work of the Standards Development Committee. It will also give genuine decision-making power to both bodies.

36.   The Working Party recommends that the Board should have the right to add projects to the Standards Development Committee's work plan, but should not have the right to remove projects from the work plan. The Standards Development Committee should seek regular guidance on its work plan from the Board. The Standards Development Committee should also discuss the main technical issues in all its proposals with the Board in depth at an early stage and as projects progress.

Standing Interpretations Committee

37.   The Working Party believes that the Standing Interpretations Committee (SIC) should continue to exist as a separate body, because neither the Board nor the Standards Development Committee would have sufficient time to develop their own Interpretations.

38.   At present, Board approval is required for a final Interpretation. Some members of the Working Party believe that this should continue. However, a majority of the Working Party would prefer final approval by the Standards Development Committee, to minimise delays in issuing Interpretations that may be needed urgently and because they believe that the SIC's own due process makes formal approval by the Board unnecessary. They propose that this should require the same majority as a decision to submit an Exposure Draft or Standard to the Board for approval (seven votes out of 11).

39.   When the SIC submits final Interpretations to the Standards Development Committee for approval, it should also send a copy to Board Members so that they can comment to the Standards Development Committee before it approves the final Interpretation.

40.   The Working Party believes that members of the SIC should be appointed by the Trustees. To avoid delays in filling vacancies on the SIC, the Working Party

recommends that the Trustees should have the power to establish a Sub-Committee for this purpose.

Consultative Group

41. The Working Party believes that IASC should maintain the Consultative Group as a useful forum for dialogue with organisations (mainly international) that have an interest in financial reporting. The Consultative Group should meet once or twice a year with the Chairmen of the Standards Development Committee, Board and Trustees and others as appropriate. The meetings should be chaired by the Chairman of the Board. The purpose of the meetings should be for the Consultative Group to:

    (a) give feedback on IASC proposals, guidance on work plan priorities and advice on relationships with key constituencies; and

    (b) receive reports on IASC's work

Members of IASC

42. The Working Party believes that the Members of IASC should continue to be the professional accountancy bodies that are members of IFAC and should continue to meet every two and a half years. The Members of IASC should meet under the Chairmanship of the Chairman of the Trustees to:

    (a) receive a report by the Trustees on their activities over the preceding two and a half years;

    (b) receive reports by the Chairmen of the Board and the Standards Development Committee on the activities, work programme and future strategy of the Board and the Standards Development Committee; and

    (c) ratify (by a simple majority of those voting) any changes to IASC's Constitution that have been approved by the Trustees and Board (see paragraph 183).

Staff

43. To play an equal role in partnership with national standard setters, IASC needs a core of high-quality technical staff (at least eight), at a central location. Some projects would be joint projects with national standard setters and staffed predominantly by the national standard setter concerned. However, IASC's own staff would need to monitor the staff work on these projects to ensure that the output meets IASC's needs.

44. The Working Party proposes that technical functions should be headed by a Technical Director, reporting to the Standards Development Committee. Commercial functions (including funding, copyright, office, equipment, communications) should be headed by a Commercial Director, reporting through the Chairman of the Standards Development Committee to the Trustees. The function of chief executive officer, currently performed by the Secretary-General, should pass to the Chairman of the Standards Development Committee.

Legal Structure

45.   The Working Party recommends that the Board should consider ways of establishing IASC as a legal entity. The Working Party also believes that IASC should investigate the possibility of seeking charitable or similar status in those countries where such status would assist fund-raising.

Timetable for Change

46.   A possible timetable for implementing the Working Party's proposals is set out in appendix 6. The Working Party recognises that this is a challenging timetable, which relies on the optimistic assumption that a provisional selection process can be largely completed before the members of IASC decide whether to approve the constitutional changes at their next meeting in May 2000.

Due Process

47.   To safeguard IASC's legitimacy, IASC's due process must ensure that International Accounting Standards are of high quality, requiring transparent and comparable information that will help participants in capital markets and others to make economic decisions, and acceptable to the users and preparers of financial statements. The Working Party believes that:

(a)   all formal discussions of the Standards Development Committee, Standing Interpretations Committee (SIC) and Board on technical issues should be open to the public. However, certain discussions (primarily selection, appointment and other personnel issues) would need to be held in private. Portions of the Trustees' meetings should also be open to the public, at the discretion of the Trustees;

(b)   IASC should make more use of new technology (such as the Internet, the web site, electronic observation of meetings), to overcome geographical barriers and the logistical problems in arranging for members of the public to attend open meetings of an international body;

(c)   IASC should publish in advance the agendas for each meeting of the Standards Development Committee, Standing Interpretations Committee, Board and Trustees and should publish promptly the decisions made at those meetings (IASC currently publishes the agenda for Board meetings in its quarterly newsletter, *Insight*, and on its web site, and publishes Board decisions immediately after each Board meeting in *Update* and SIC decisions in *News from the SIC*); and

(d)   when IASC publishes a Standard, it should continue its recently adopted practice of publishing a Basis for Conclusions to explain publicly how it reached its conclusions and to give background information that may help users of IASC standards to apply them in practice. IASC should also publish dissentient opinions (IASC's current Constitution prohibits this).

48.   The Working Party believes that the Standards Development Committee should make use of the following, although there should be no requirement to do so for every project:

(a)   'public hearings' to discuss proposed standards; and

(b)   field tests (both in developed countries and in emerging markets) to ensure that proposals are practical and workable.

Where practicable, public hearings and field tests should be co-ordinated with national standard setters.

49.   An important objective of the Working Party's model is closer co-ordination between IASC's due process and the due process of national standard setters, who will necessarily remain autonomous. The Working Party recognises that many national standard setters will not give up their own due process, nor can they give an irrevocable undertaking that they will tie themselves completely on every project to IASC's due process. However, the Working Party believes that IASC should aim to integrate IASC's due process more closely with national due process. This is something that will probably not happen overnight but will occur gradually as the relationship between IASC and national standard setters evolves. The Working Party's desired outcome is the following procedure for most, and preferably all, projects that have international implications:

(a)   IASC and national standard setters would co-ordinate their work plans so that when IASC starts a project, national standard setters would also add it to their own work plans so that they can play a full part in developing an international consensus. Similarly, where national standard setters start projects, IASC would consider whether it needs to develop a new Standard or revise its existing Standards;

(b)   IASC and national standard setters would co-ordinate their timetables so that national standard setters would aim to publish their own proposals at the same time as IASC proposals and so that the results from national exposure are available in time for IASC to consider, and vice versa. IASC may need, in certain cases, to slow down its own timetable to some extent so that national standard setters can satisfy their own due process requirements. However, to avoid giving national standard setters a veto in IASC's process, IASC would sometimes need to issue its own proposals without significant delay, even if some national standard setters were not yet ready to issue their own proposals;

(c)   members of the Standards Development Committee would not be required to vote for an IASC treatment in their national standard setters, since each country would remain free to adopt IASC standards with amendments or to adopt other standards. However, the existence of an international consensus is clearly one factor that members of national standard setters would consider when they decide how to vote on national standards;

(d)   IASC would continue to publish its own Exposure Drafts and other documents for public comment;

(e)   national standard setters would publish their own Exposure Drafts at approximately the same time as IASC Exposure Drafts and would seek specific comments on any significant divergences between the two Exposure Drafts. The Working Party expects that market forces would make such divergences increasingly rare. In some instances, national standard setters may ask for specific comments on issues of particular relevance to their country or include more detailed guidance than is included in an International Accounting Standard; and

(f)   national standard setters would follow their own full due process, which they would, ideally, choose to integrate with IASC's due process. Issues arising would be considered by national standard setters. This integration would avoid unnecessary delays in completing standards and would also minimise the likelihood of unnecessary differences between the standards that result. In the same way as for Exposure Drafts, the Working Party expects that it will become increasingly rare for national standard setters to adopt standards that differ from International Accounting Standards.

50.   The Working Party believes that there is now a case for IASC to extend its comment periods for Exposure Drafts and other documents. A minimum of four months may be appropriate, although particularly complex or controversial issues may warrant longer comment periods.

51.   IASC has recently published German and Russian translations of its standards and is working on a Polish translation. These are the first translations that IASC has undertaken. The Working Party recommends that IASC should publish or promote translations of its standards into other languages, preferably on a self-financing basis. The objective of such translations is to:

(a)   promote the use of International Accounting Standards;

(b)   ensure that users of International Accounting Standards have access to high quality translations; and

(c)   raise revenue.

52.   The Working Party believes that IASC should explore ways of establishing quality control of translations published by others, possibly by working with local standard setters and accountancy bodies.

Implementation, Enforcement and Training

53.   The Working Party believes that it is not the role of IASC to review national standards in order to assess actively whether those national standards result in compliance with International Accounting Standards.

54.   In the Working Party's view, identifying and dealing with departures by preparers from International Accounting Standards (or from national requirements that are consistent with International Accounting Standards) is primarily a matter for auditors, professional accountancy bodies, IFAC, national enforcement agencies and supranational bodies such as IOSCO and the Basle Committee. IASC does not have the resources to do this effectively. Also, IASC lacks both legal authority to take action and legal protection from those who dispute alleged departures.

55.   The Working Party believes that IASC should give advice to national regulators and other enforcement agencies in their efforts to enforce national standards that comply with International Accounting Standards, but only if the regulator in question both:

    (a)   pays for the advice on a fully self-financing basis; and

    (b)   gives IASC satisfactory indemnities against legal action by those who dispute alleged departures.

56.   The Working Party believes that IASC should consider publishing training material, illustrative examples and other implementation guidance, such as staff bulletins and, perhaps, also giving training courses.   The Working Party believes that IASC should not provide a technical enquiry service.

Funding

57.   The current method of funding IASC is open to a number of criticisms:

    (a)   although international travel and the need to research issues in an international context suggest a need for substantial resources, IASC's resources are remarkably modest. This leads to disproportionate demands on the time of Board Representatives, Technical Advisors and the staff;

    (b)   there is a conflict between the promotion of IAS (especially in poorer countries) and the need to raise funds ('the user pays'). For example, IASC's policy of charging for Exposure Drafts may deter comments;

    (c)   existing sources of revenue could be threatened by increased use of the Internet and by the increasing availability of national standards that are identical to, or very closely based on, International Accounting Standards;

    (d)   donations may undermine IASC's actual or perceived independence;

    (e)   there is a lack of geographical balance in corporate donations. As a result, it may appear that IASC gives more weight to the views of countries that provide a higher level of donations;

    (f)   IASC relies on volatile and uncertain sources of funding. This inhibits long-term planning, diverts scarce staff time and makes it difficult to recruit permanent staff;

    (g)   the direct and indirect cost of Board seats deters developing and emerging countries from applying to join the Board;

    (h)   the limitations of IASC's resources have forced it to prioritise projects aimed primarily at the needs of developed countries and to pay less attention to identifying and meeting any specific needs of developing countries and of countries in East and Central Europe and in Asia that are in transition from centrally planned economies to market driven economies; and

    (i)   many organisations (including accountancy bodies that are not on the Board, stock exchanges, governments and national standard setters and others) benefit from IASC's work but do not provide funding. Also, the fact that IASC's only members are professional accountancy bodies is an impediment to fund-raising in some countries.

58.   Preferably, IASC would need to increase its annual funding to around £5 million at current prices to implement the Working Party's proposals. This amount excludes costs that, under the Working Party's proposals, would be borne by national standard setters and others. These costs would amount to between, perhaps, £1 million and £1.5 million. The amount of £5 million also excludes time costs for volunteers.

59.   The Working Party believes that IASC needs more secure funding based on a formula, not a constant money drive, so as not to divert Trustee and staff time. There may be a need to use different formulas in different countries. There are several different ways of raising national contributions:

(a)   directly from Board members (including perhaps observers) and/or Members of IASC;

(b)   from a variety of groups in each country who benefit from IASC's work (e.g. preparers, users, regulators, the accountancy profession); or

(c)   indirectly from groups who benefit from IASC's work, with Trustees and/or Members of IASC in each country taking responsibility for collecting the contributions for their countries. For example, it may be desirable to have some degree of commitment to funding over some minimum period, perhaps through organisations in each larger country, to facilitate longer-term planning.

60.   The Working Party supports the general principle that those who benefit from IASC's work should pay for its work. The beneficiaries include users of financial statements, business enterprises, auditors, the accountancy profession in general, stock exchanges, regulators, central banks, governments and other government and intergovernmental agencies. However, it is not easy to identify all of those who benefit from IASC's work or to devise a fair way of sharing the cost between the different groups of beneficiaries. The Working Party would welcome suggestions on this.

61.   In looking at various funding models, the Working Party considered a number of points, including the following:

(a)   the enterprises that gain the greatest financial benefit from IASC's work are listed enterprises. Therefore, stock exchanges should be an important source of funding. It would seem equitable that all stock exchanges should contribute on a collective basis to remove the incentive for some stock exchanges to be 'free riders' – benefiting from IASC's work without paying for it;

(b)   Trustees or member bodies could, perhaps, act as agents for fund-raising in their own countries/constituencies, working to targets agreed to be fair;

(c)   representation of a broad range of constituencies on the Standards Development Committee, Board and Foundation should help fund-raising, as constituents will be more willing to fund a process in which they have representation;

(d)   IASC may be able to persuade enterprises to endow IASC with permanent capital, as a source of investment income to fund part or all of IASC's work;

(e)   without a fair and equitable agreement for sharing publications revenue, publications revenue might drop if national standard setters adopted IAS and companies looked to national requirements instead of to IASC pronouncements;

(f)   by co-operating on projects on a rotational basis, national standard setters may save substantial costs overall. Therefore, it would be reasonable for national standard setters to devote significant resources to the Standards Development Committee (salary of the individual serving on the Standards Development Committee, travel costs, staff support, space, communications);

(g)   professional accountancy bodies carry out the standard setting role in many countries. Some of them may be reluctant to finance an international body when the majority of their local members do not operate in the international arena, as those local members may not realise how international co-operation leverages the resources that are available for standard-setting. However, they may be able to contribute funding not only in cash but also through secondments and through outsourcing of work to them; and

(h)   developing countries are unlikely to have the resources to pay a full contribution towards the cost of IASC. However, although any contribution structure is likely to include a subsidy from more established economies, this is likely to be in the public interest and in the interests of both developing and more established economies. Bodies such as the United Nations and the International Finance Corporation may be willing to support translations of International Accounting Standards and other work by IASC for emerging markets. They may also be willing to fund part of the cost of a Board seat for developing countries as IFAC does at present.

62.   The Working Party sees merit in a funding model that relies more or less equally on funding from a number of reasonably well-defined groups. An example would be a model that looks to the accountancy profession, government and the business community to provide roughly equal proportions of IASC's funding. The most effective and efficient way to collect the business community's contribution might be through stock exchanges. The Working Party recognises that funding is a vital issue and aims to develop a more detailed funding plan during the period for public comment on this Discussion Paper. In the meantime, the Working Party would welcome comments on funding.

Conclusion

63.   The completion of IASC's current work programme to develop the IOSCO core standards is now imminent. However, IASC will face even greater challenges as it works, in partnership with national standard setters, for further convergence between national standards. Therefore, it is vital to give IASC the right structure for the beginning of the twenty-first century. The Working Party invites all parties affected by accounting standards to play a full part in this important debate.

INVITATION TO COMMENT

The Working Party welcomes comments on the questions set out below and on any other aspects of its proposals.   If commentators put forward other proposals, the Working Party would like them to explain how their proposals satisfy the objectives identified by the Working Party.

Comments should be submitted in writing so as to be received by **30 April 1999**. All replies will be put on public record unless confidentiality is requested by the commentator. Comments should be addressed to:

The Secretary-General
International Accounting Standards Committee
166 Fleet Street
London EC4A 2DY
United Kingdom

Fax: +44 (171) 353-0562
E-mail: CommentLetters@iasc.org.uk

If commentators respond by fax or E-mail, it would be helpful if they could also send a hard copy of their response by post.

The Working Party particularly welcomes answers to the following questions, with reasons for those answers.

Objectives

Q1.   Do you agree that it is important to focus IASC's objectives more precisely as follows:

  (a)   to develop International Accounting Standards that require high-quality, transparent and comparable information which will help participants in capital markets and others to make economic decisions; and

  (b)   to promote the use of International Accounting Standards by working with national standard setters to:

   (i)   bring about convergence, for listed enterprises (i.e. enterprises with publicly traded equity or debt securities) and other economically significant enterprises, between national accounting standards and International Accounting Standards; and

   (ii)   encourage national, regional and international authorities to permit or require unlisted enterprises that, individually, are not economically significant to use those International Accounting Standards if those Standards meet the needs of the users of the financial statements of such enterprises.

These proposed comments should be read in the light of the Working Party's comments on the focus of IASC's work. Do you have any comments on the focus of IASC's work? (see paragraphs 28-70)

Structure of IASC - Key Issues

Q2. The Working Party has identified the following key issues that must be addressed to give IASC a structure that will enable it to continue meeting its objectives:

(a) partnership with national standard setters - IASC should enter into a partnership with national standard setters so that IASC can work together with them to accelerate convergence between national standards and International Accounting Standards around solutions requiring high-quality, transparent and comparable information that will help participants in capital markets and others to make economic decisions;

(b) wider participation in the IASC Board - a wider group of countries and organisations should take part in the IASC Board, without diluting the quality of the Board's work; and

(c) appointment - the process for appointments to the IASC Board and key IASC committees should be the responsibility of a variety of constituencies, while ensuring that those appointed are competent, independent and objective.

Do you agree that these are the key issues to be addressed in developing an effective structure for IASC? (see paragraphs 112-123)   The Working Party's proposals for improving IASC's due process are discussed separately below (see Question 6).

Structure of IASC - Addressing the Key Issues

Q3. The Working Party's proposals address these key issues by the following changes:

(a) a partnership with national standard setters:

(i) Steering Committees would be replaced by a Standards Development Committee, on which national standard setters would play a major role in developing International Accounting Standards. The Standards Development Committee would also be responsible for approving the publication of final SIC Interpretations prepared by the Standing Interpretations Committee; and

(ii) the Standards Development Committee would be supported by a Standards Development Advisory Committee, which would act as a channel of communication with those national standard setters who are unable to participate directly in the Standards Development Committee because of its limited size;

(b) wider participation in the IASC Board - the Board would have a wider membership than at present. The Board would still be responsible for the final approval of International Accounting Standards and Exposure Drafts; and

(c) appointment - the Advisory Council would be replaced by Trustees. Among other things, the Trustees would appoint members of the Standards Development Committee, the Board and the Standing Interpretations Committee. The Trustees would also have responsibility for monitoring IASC's effectiveness and for finance.

These proposals are set out in paragraphs 124-200 and summarised in tables 1 and 2 on pages 12 to 17 and in Figures 1 and 2 on pages 18 and 19.

Do you support the Working Party's proposals? Should any changes be made to these proposals? Should the Working Party consider any other ways of meeting the needs identified above? If commentators put forward other proposals, the Working Party would like them to explain how their proposals satisfy the objectives identified by the Working Party.

Approval of International Accounting Standards

Q4. The Working Party considered a range of different ways of specifying the respective powers of the Standards Development Committee and the Board. Among these were:

(a)   positive approval required by a majority or super-majority of the Board for all International Accounting Standards and Exposure Drafts;

(b)   the Board (or perhaps a specified majority or a specified minority of the Board) has the power to reject proposed International Accounting Standards and Exposure Drafts;

(c)   the Board (or perhaps a specified majority or a specified minority of the Board) has the power to return proposed International Accounting Standards and Exposure Drafts to the Standards Development Committee for re-consideration, but not to reject them indefinitely; and

(d)   the Standards Development Committee must consult the Board, but the Board has no power to delay or reject International Accounting Standards or Exposure Drafts.

Individual members of the Working Party have preferences for different points in this range. Some members of the Working Party prefer option (a) above. Other members of the Working Party prefer option (d) above. However, the Working Party believes that the precise voting arrangements are less important than the need for the Standards Development Committee and the Board to work together constructively.

The Working Party believes that a constructive attitude of close and effective co-operation is a striking feature of the current Board and of IASC's Committees. Consequently, the Working Party is confident that the Standards Development Committee and the Board will achieve the close and effective relationship that will be needed.

The Working Party proposes that the publication of a Standard or Exposure Draft should require approval by 60% of the Board (15 votes out of 25). At present, an Exposure Draft requires a positive vote by two thirds of the Board; a final Standard requires a positive vote by three quarters of the Board. The Working Party further concluded that the Chairman of the Board should be required to ensure that the Board considers and votes on proposed Exposure Drafts and Standards submitted by the Standards Development Committee within three months of receipt or, if later, at its next meeting.

If the Board rejects a proposed Exposure Draft or Standard, the Board should send the document back to the Standards Development Committee for further consideration, giving public reasons for its rejection. After considering the reasons given by the Board, the Standards Development Committee may decide to:

(a)   prepare a revised proposal and submit it to the Board for approval in the normal way; or

(b)   resubmit its original proposal to the Board:

    (i)   if nine or more members of the Standards Development Committee have voted to resubmit the same proposal, Board approval should require a simple majority (13 votes out of 25); and

    (ii)   if seven or eight members of the Standards Development Committee have voted to resubmit the proposal, the proposal should be treated in the same way as a new proposal. In other words, Board approval should require the normal 60% majority (i.e. 15 votes out of 25).

At present, each delegation has one vote. This means that Board delegations are sometimes forced to abstain where the members of the delegation are unable to agree among themselves. Given the current requirement for a positive vote by three quarters of the Board, an abstention is effectively the same as a vote against a Standard. This might suggest that each member of the delegation should be given an individual vote, to reduce the risk of deadlock. However, discussions among, say, 50 voting individuals would be much more cumbersome than discussions among 50 individuals representing 25 voting delegations. The Working Party recommends that IASC should retain the current practice that each delegation has one vote.

The Working Party believes that the Board should not have the power to amend proposed Exposure Drafts and Standards submitted by the Standards Development Committee.

The Working Party believes that these proposals will ensure reasonably widespread acceptance for IASC's work, without undue risk of paralysing the work of the Standards Development Committee. This will also give genuine decision-making power to both bodies.

Do you support this proposal (see paragraphs 164-178)?

Under the Working Party's proposal, positive approval by the Board would still be required for all International Accounting Standards and Exposure Drafts. Do you agree that such Board approval should be required? Or do you believe that the Board should have no power to delay or reject Standards or Drafts?

If you do not support the proposal set out in paragraphs 164-178, please indicate what changes should be made and explain how your proposal will address the following three crucial considerations:

(a)   the need to convince users, preparers and IASC's other constituents that IASC's standards will meet their needs;

(b)   the need to attract suitably qualified individuals to serve on the Standards Development Committee and the Board; and

(c)   the need for the Standards Development Committee and the Board to work together closely and effectively for the public interest.

Approval of SIC Interpretations

Q5. At present, Board approval is required for a final Interpretation. Do you agree that:

(a) a SIC final Interpretation should require approval by the Standards Development Committee, and that approval by the Board should no longer be required; and

(b) the approval of a final Interpretation should require the same majority in the Standards Development Committee as a decision to submit an Exposure Draft or Standard to the Board for approval (seven votes out of 11)?

Should any other changes be made to the structure or operations of the SIC (see paragraphs 96-99 and 184-189)?

Due Process

Q6. Should any changes be made to IASC's due process (see paragraphs 108-110 and 201-214)? In particular, should IASC:

(a) open all discussions of the proposed Standards Development Committee, Standing Interpretations Committee and Board on technical issues to the public;

(b) open portions of Trustees' meetings to the public, at the discretion of the Trustees;

(c) make more use of new technology, such as the Internet, the web site, and electronic observation of open meetings;

(d) publish in advance the agendas for each meeting of the Standards Development Committee, Standing Interpretations Committee, Board and Trustees and publish promptly the decisions made at those meetings (IASC currently publishes the agenda for Board meetings in its quarterly newsletter, *Insight*, and on its web site. IASC also publishes Board decisions immediately after each Board meeting in *Update* and SIC decisions in *News from the SIC*);

(e) publish a Basis for Conclusions with its Standards;

(f) publish with its Standards any dissentient opinions (i.e. statements explaining why one or more Board Members or members of the Standards Development Committee voted against the Standards);

(g) hold public hearings for some or all projects (without a requirement to do so in every case);

(h) carry out field tests of some or all of its proposals (without a requirement to do so in every case);

(i) publish translations of International Accounting Standards (as well as other documents, such as Exposure Drafts);

(j) ask Members of IASC, or others, to control the quality of those translations that IASC does not publish itself;

(k)   lengthen comment periods for Exposure Drafts and other documents;

(l)   distribute Exposure Drafts (and other documents issued for comment) without charge, if it is financially feasible to do so; or

(m)   make other changes to its due process (please specify these changes)?

Implementation, Enforcement and Training

Q7.   Should IASC:

(a)   be more pro-active in reviewing national standards in order to assess whether those national standards result in compliance with International Accounting Standards;

(b)   give advice to national regulators and other enforcement agencies in their efforts to enforce national standards that comply with International Accounting Standards, but only if the regulator in question both:

(i)   pays for the advice on a fully self-financing basis; and

(ii)   gives IASC satisfactory indemnities against legal action by those who dispute alleged departures;

(c)   be more pro-active in identifying departures from International Accounting Standards and reporting those departures to national enforcement agencies, supranational bodies such as IOSCO or the Basle Committee, IFAC or IASC's own Member bodies;

(d)   publish training material, illustrative examples and other implementation guidance, such as staff bulletins;

(e)   introduce a technical enquiry service;

(f)   hold training courses (if you think that IASC should provide training, please specify whether such courses should be self-financing); or

(g)   do anything else to improve the implementation, enforcement and training of International Accounting Standards?

These issues are discussed in paragraphs 215-220.

Funding

The Working Party recognises that funding is a vital issue and aims to develop a more detailed funding plan during the period for public comment on this Discussion Paper.

Q8.   Should IASC make any changes to the way in which it is funded? (paragraphs 221-235)

Do you support a funding model that relies more or less equally on funding from a number of reasonably well-defined groups? If you support such a model, which groups should participate in the funding and on what basis? An example would be a model that looks to the accountancy profession, government and the business community to provide roughly equal proportions of IASC's funding.

Do you have any other suggestions for funding IASC?

Other Comments

Q9.   Do you have any other comments on the structure of IASC?

Contents

Contents

1. INTRODUCTION

1.   The International Accounting Standards Committee (IASC) is an independent private sector body formed in 1973 through an agreement made by professional accountancy bodies from Australia, Canada, France, Germany, Japan, Mexico, the Netherlands, the United Kingdom and Ireland and the United States of America. Since 1983, IASC's Members have been all the professional accountancy bodies that are Members of the International Federation of Accountants (IFAC). As at 1 November 1998, IASC and IFAC have 143 Members in 103 countries.

2.   IASC was founded to formulate and publish, in the public interest, International Accounting Standards to be observed in the presentation of published financial statements and to promote their worldwide acceptance and observance. It was envisaged that International Accounting Standards should be capable of worldwide acceptance and contribute to a significant improvement in the quality and comparability of corporate disclosure. This vision has not changed since 1973 and there is no reason why it should change in the foreseeable future.

3.   IASC has issued over 30 International Accounting Standards. These standards deal with topics that affect the financial statements of business enterprises. The Board has also issued a Framework for the Preparation and Presentation of Financial Statements, which helps the Board to achieve conceptual consistency within International Accounting Standards. The Framework states that its purpose is, among other things, to assist the Board in:

(a)   developing new International Accounting Standards and in reviewing existing International Accounting Standards; and

(b)   promoting the harmonisation of regulations, accounting standards and procedures relating to the presentation of financial statements by providing a basis for reducing the number of alternative accounting treatments permitted by International Accounting Standards.

4.   International Accounting Standards have done a great deal both to improve and to harmonise financial reporting around the world. They are used:

(a)   as a basis for national accounting requirements in many countries;

(b)   as an international benchmark by some countries that develop their own requirements (including certain major industrialised countries, regional organisations such as the European Union, and an increasing number of emerging markets such as China and many other countries in Asia, Central Europe and the countries of the former Soviet Union);

(c)   by stock exchanges and regulatory authorities that allow foreign or domestic companies to present financial statements in accordance with International Accounting Standards;

(d)   by supra-national bodies that rely on IASC to produce accounting standards that improve the quality of financial reporting and the comparability of financial statements, instead of developing their own requirements;

(e)   by the World Bank Group and other development agencies that require borrowers and recipients of other forms of aid to follow high standards of financial reporting and accountability; and

(f)   by a growing number of individual companies.

5.   IASC has been successful in developing high quality International Accounting Standards that have gained increasing acceptance around the world. To build on that achievement, the Working Party believes that IASC should now be anticipating future needs and modifying its own role and structure in response to major changes in the environment in which IASC operates. Some of these changes have been driven by external factors, while others have been driven partly by IASC's own achievements.

6.   The changing role of IASC creates new challenges and opportunities for IASC. Although IASC's existing structure has served it well, the Working Party believes that IASC needs to change its structure so that it can meet these new challenges, and seize those opportunities, as effectively as it has responded to other challenges and opportunities in the first 25 years of its life.

7.   Section 2 of this Paper discusses the changes in IASC's environment and the new challenges that these changes create for IASC. Section 3 reviews IASC's objectives and section 4 summarises IASC's current structure and due process. Section 5 develops a model for strengthening IASC's structure and due process to keep pace with the changes in the environment. Section 6 deals with implementation, enforcement and training issues. Last, and far from least, section 7 looks at how IASC's funding can be improved.

2. NEW CHALLENGES FOR IASC

8. For the first 25 years of its existence, IASC has mainly been a harmoniser - a body that selects an accounting treatment that already exists at the national level in some countries and then seeks worldwide acceptance of that treatment, perhaps with some modifications. IASC's current structure has enabled IASC to play an effective role as a harmoniser.

9. In recent years, IASC has taken on a more innovatory role in certain areas. For example, in March 1997, IASC's Steering Committee on Financial Instruments published proposals for dealing with financial assets and financial liabilities and those proposals went beyond any requirements or proposals that existed at a national level.

10. The pace of change in business life and the financial world is accelerating rapidly. The Working Party believes that in the future IASC will need to be an innovator and an initiator to a much greater extent than it is today. IASC can meet this challenge only by working closely with national standard setters.

11. Another increasingly important challenge for IASC will be to work with national standard setters to bring about convergence between national accounting standards and International Accounting Standards around solutions requiring listed enterprises (i.e. enterprises with publicly traded equity or debt securities) and other economically significant enterprises to report high-quality, transparent and comparable information that will help participants in capital markets and others to make economic decisions. The standards of many countries are already converging with International Accounting Standards. However, trends such as globalisation and the increasing pace of business and financial change have made this task more urgent. The Working Party believes that IASC and national standard setters need to find new ways of working together to minimise unnecessary delays in reaching consensus and implementing the results of that consensus.

CHANGES IN IASC'S ENVIRONMENT

12. In the Working Party's view, the new challenges facing IASC result from significant changes in IASC's environment in recent years. The most important of these changes are:

    (a) a rapid growth in international capital markets, combined with an increase in cross-border listings and cross-border investment. These have led to efforts by securities regulators to develop a common "passport" for cross-border securities listings and to achieve greater comparability in financial reporting;

    (b) efforts of global organisations (such as the World Trade Organisation) and regional bodies (such as the European Union, NAFTA, MERCOSUR and APEC) to dismantle barriers to international world trade;

    (c) a trend towards the internationalisation of business regulation;

    (d) increasing influence of International Accounting Standards on national accounting requirements and practice;

    (e) accelerating innovation in business transactions;

(f)   increasing demand from users for new types of financial and other performance information;

(g)   new developments in the electronic distribution of financial and other performance information; and

(h)   growing need for relevant and reliable financial and other performance information both in countries in transition from planned economies to market economies and in developing and newly industrialised economies.

13.   These changes are discussed below. They have placed strain on the organisational and financial resources of a body that relies, as IASC does, extensively on work by volunteers and on relatively informal contacts with national standard setters.

International Capital Markets

14.   In recent years, there has been explosive growth in the provision of international capital, in the opportunities for international investment and in the number and size of international securities offerings, as shown by the table set out below. This has fuelled a demand for a core set of high-quality International Accounting Standards that business enterprises from all countries can use when they seek access to the international capital markets. This has brought an increase in cross-border listings and cross-border investment. It has also led to demand for greater comparability in accounting and disclosure practices.

Cross-Border Transactions in Bonds and Equities As a Percentage of Gross Domestic Product (GDP) (Gross purchases and sales of securities between residents and non-residents)

	1975	1980	1985	1990	1995	1997
United States	4	9	35	89	135	213
Japan	2	8	62	119	65	96
Germany	5	7	33	57	172	253
France	-	5	21	54	187	313
Italy	1	1	4	27	253	672
Canada	3	9	27	65	189	358

Source: Table V.1, Bank for International Settlements, 68th Annual Report (1998)

15.   The acceptance by stock exchanges of International Accounting Standards brings great benefits to users of financial statements and to business enterprises that report under International Accounting Standards:

(a)   users benefit by having high-quality financial information that is comparable from one enterprise to another, comprehensive and readily comprehensible; and

(b)   enterprises benefit by having access to a larger pool of foreign capital at a lower cost and by saving the cost of preparing reconciliation statements to another set of accounting standards for cross-border listings. Also, the increasing convergence of national standards (through convergence with International Accounting Standards) reduces the need to restate financial information for consolidation purposes.

16. Many stock exchanges accept International Accounting Standards for cross-border listing purposes, but stock exchanges in Canada, Japan and the United States are currently exceptions. IASC has therefore adopted a work programme to produce a comprehensive core set of high quality standards, aiming at more general acceptance of International Accounting Standards for cross-border listings. The Technical Committee of the International Organization of Securities Commissions (IOSCO) has agreed that when IASC completes the work programme to the Technical Committee's satisfaction, the Technical Committee will consider recommending that IOSCO should endorse International Accounting Standards for cross-border capital raising and listing purposes in all global markets. IASC aims to complete the core standards in 1998.

17. If IOSCO endorses International Accounting Standards (and International Standards on Auditing), there is likely to be a substantial increase in the credibility of financial statements prepared under International Accounting Standards and audited under International Standards on Auditing.

18. Some commentators believe that capital markets are moving towards becoming not national capital markets but part of a single global capital market. Illustrations of this development are:

   (a) the development of international securities trading over the Internet;

   (b) recent cross-border alliances between national stock exchanges; and

   (c) the creation of EASDAQ, a pan-European over-the-counter market.

   These commentators believe that movement towards a single global capital market will inevitably lead to demands for securities and stock market regulation to move from the national arena to the international arena and for a similar development in the process for setting accounting standards.

19. At present, enterprises with cross-border listings sometimes have to report under two different accounting regimes. In a number of well-publicised cases, such enterprises have reported substantially different information under the two regimes. This has caused confusion for users of that financial information. The reporting of such significant differences may cause even greater confusion as the circle of cross-border investors becomes wider.

World Trade

20. Global and regional organisations and initiatives (such as the World Trade Organisation, the OECD, the European Union, NAFTA, MERCOSUR and APEC) are making great efforts to liberalise international trade. These efforts have stimulated international trade and also added impetus to the trend of globalisation that is apparent in many sectors. The result is a growing demand for business enterprises to present relevant, reliable, comparable and comprehensible financial information to users in other countries. Several of these bodies are looking to IASC to produce standards that will satisfy this demand. For example:

   (a) at the World Trade Organisation conference in 1996, government ministers issued a statement in 1996 encouraging "the successful completion of international standards in the accountancy sector by IASC, IFAC and IOSCO";

(b)   the European Commission announced in 1995 that, rather than create a European Accounting Standards Board or a new layer of European Accounting Standards, it would associate the European Union with the efforts undertaken by IASC and IOSCO towards a broader international harmonisation of accounting standards. The European Commission plays a leading role in co-ordinating the development of financial reporting in the European Union; and

(c)   the Business Forum of the Asia Pacific Economic Co-operation (APEC) countries gave support in 1996 to the internationalisation of accounting through a core of consistent high quality International Accounting Standards that would be acceptable for general purpose accounting guidelines in all APEC countries.

21.   Convergence of national accounting standards will make it easier for public accountants to practise across national borders. This will add to competition in accountancy services and may reduce their cost.

Internationalisation of Business Regulation

22.   Many business activities are subject to supervision by government regulatory agencies. Increasingly, these agencies are looking to develop co-ordinated international approaches to supervision through bodies such as IOSCO, the Basle Committee on Banking Supervision and the International Association of Insurance Supervisors. International co-operation on supervisory matters is likely to increase in response to the recent turmoil in many financial markets. In a number of cases, regulatory and supervisory requirements rely on information in financial statements. Such requirements are likely to be more effective if they are based on consistent application of uniform accounting requirements.

National Accounting Standards

23.   The prospect of IOSCO endorsement and the growing international support for IASC have given national standard setters increasing incentives to bring their own requirements into line with International Accounting Standards. As a result, many countries have already adopted International Accounting Standards or are in the process of bringing their domestic standards into line with International Accounting Standards. In addition, many companies from countries whose accounting standards are not widely recognised have chosen to adopt International Accounting Standards. This trend has raised IASC's profile and increased the interest in its work. IASC's work now has a great impact on many more groups, in many more countries, than before. These groups now want to participate in IASC's decisions.

24.   Several national standard setters have stated publicly that they accept the need for, and are committed to, international harmonisation. For example:

(a)   in their Policy Statement 6, International Harmonisation Policy, the Australian Accounting Standards Board (AASB) and the Public Sector Accounting Standards Board (PSASB) state that their objective is to pursue the development of an internationally accepted set of accounting standards which can be adopted in Australia. Their interim objective is to work towards ensuring that compliance with Australian Accounting Standards results in compliance with International Accounting Standards;

(b)   a Task Force on Standard Setting set up by the Canadian Institute of Chartered Accountants reported in May 1998 that "the internationalization of standard setting for private sector accounting and auditing is inevitable". One long term goal set out in the Task Force's report was as follows. "There will be one set of internationally-accepted accounting standards in the private sector. Canada will play a significant role in establishing international accounting standards and retain its authority to set unique Canadian Accounting Standards where circumstances warrant";

(c)   the Chairman of the UK's Accounting Standards Board wrote in his Progress Report for 1997 that "the Board has adopted a policy that combines a sincere commitment to work for international harmonisation with the flexibility to ensure that each issue is evaluated with full regard to the needs of financial reporting in the UK and the Republic of Ireland"; and

(d)   one objective set out in the strategic plan of the USA's Financial Accounting Standards Board (FASB) is to promote the development and acceptance of a superior set of international accounting standards.

25.   An important recent development in Europe is new legislation in Belgium, France, Germany and Italy that allows some domestic companies to use International Accounting Standards instead of domestic standards in their consolidated financial statements, subject to certain conditions. Other countries in the European Union are considering similar measures.

26.   These European countries will still permit or require some enterprises to use existing domestic requirements instead of International Accounting Standards. In time, the desire for comparability within individual countries may create pressure for those domestic requirements to converge towards International Accounting Standards.

27.   In the National Securities Markets Improvements Act of 1996, the US Congress stated that the "establishment of a high-quality comprehensive set of generally accepted international accounting standards would greatly facilitate international financing activities and, most significantly, would enhance the ability of foreign corporations to access and list in the United States markets". It called on the Securities and Exchange Commission (SEC) to "enhance its vigorous support for the development of high-quality international accounting standards as soon as practicable".

Innovation in Business Transactions

28.   Business and finance are becoming more complex with the result that accounting standards have had to deal with more complex issues. Prominent examples are the growth of trading in derivatives and the increasing use of securitisation transactions. IASC has dealt with this increased complexity by, for example, improving its research before developing new and revised Standards, consulting specialists, improving its due process, and sharing resources with national standard setting bodies. The complexities and controversies will undoubtedly continue and IASC must make sure that it is in a position to address them effectively.

Demand for New Types of Financial and Other Performance Information

29.   Increasingly, users of financial statements are calling for information that is not easily captured by traditional accounting techniques. For example, as the service sector becomes more prominent in many economies, users are starting to ask for information about human resources and intangible assets. Similarly, growing concern for environmental issues is leading to requests for more comprehensive reporting in this area. IASC will need to draw on greater research and innovation capability (either its own or that of national standard setters) to deal with these emerging topics effectively.

Electronic Distribution of Information

30.   Enterprises are beginning to use channels such as the Internet and CD-ROMs to distribute financial and other performance information more quickly and in greater volume. The availability of greater computing power is also making it feasible to generate information of a kind or quality that was not available only a few years ago. In time, enterprises may be reporting on a real-time basis. This trend may call for changes in the nature of financial reporting standards. Also, standard setters may need to find new mechanisms for responding quickly to new reporting practices stemming from the rapid innovation in information technology.

Countries in Transition and Developing and Newly Industrialised Countries

31.   Several countries in East and Central Europe and in Asia are in transition from centrally planned economies to market driven economies. This change has led to a need for new national accounting requirements. Many of these countries have looked, or are looking, to International Accounting Standards as the basis for their new national accounting standards.

32.   Many developing and newly industrialised countries are using International Accounting Standards as their national requirements, or as the basis for their national requirements. These countries have a growing need for relevant and reliable financial information to meet the requirements both of domestic users and of international providers of the capital that they need.

33.   International Accounting Standards help borrowers and recipients of aid to meet the strict accountability required by the World Bank and other development and aid agencies.

34.   IASC liaises closely with intergovernmental bodies that seek to improve accounting practices in countries in transition and in developing and newly industrialising countries. These include:

(a)   the World Bank Group;

(b)   the United Nations Conference on Trade and Development (UNCTAD) and UNCTAD's Intergovernmental Working Group of Experts on International Standards of Accounting and Reporting (ISAR); and

(c)   the Organisation for Economic Co-operation and Development (OECD).

IMPACT OF THESE ENVIRONMENTAL CHANGES ON IASC

35.   The trends discussed above show a clear and growing demand from the market for high-quality global accounting standards that provide transparency and comparability. Indeed, in October 1998

    (a)   the G-22 Working Party on Transparency and Accountability reported that: "weaknesses in the provision and use of information played a major part in the development and spread of recent international financial crises." The report called for " a set of high quality, internationally acceptable accounting standards"; and

    (b)   a declaration of G7 Finance Ministers and Central Bank Governors on 30 October stated, among other things: "We call upon (...) the IASC to finalise by early 1999 a proposal for a full range of internationally agreed accounting standards. IOSCO, IAIS, and the Basle Committee should complete a timely review of these standards. (...) We commit ourselves to endeavour to ensure that private sector institutions in our countries comply with these principles, standards and codes of best practice. We call upon (...) all countries which participate in global capital markets similarly to commit to comply with these internationally agreed codes and standards (...)"

Similarly, the Chairman of the Basle Committee on Banking Supervision has stated that "the Basle Committee considers transparency to be a key element of an effectively supervised, safe and sound banking system".

36.   IASC's international structure and record of success have put it in a unique position to satisfy the demand for high-quality global accounting standards. However, IASC cannot take further success for granted. Among other things, IASC's role in the future is unlikely to be the same as in the past. In its early years, IASC acted mainly as a consolidator of existing national standards. In more recent times, it has begun to combine that role with the role of a catalyst - a co-ordinator of national initiatives and an initiator of new work at the national level. In the future, IASC's role as a catalyst and initiator should become more prominent.

37.   Another important consideration is the vastly increased significance of IASC's work. IASC's structure worked well when IASC's work affected a relatively small number of countries and enterprises. There is no guarantee that this structure will work without modification at a time when IASC's work has a direct or indirect effect in almost every country.

38.   As explained above, innovation in business transactions is accelerating, demand from users for new types of financial and other performance information is increasing and there are rapid developments in electronic distribution of information. Also, the life cycle of standards in all fields – not just in accounting – is shrinking rapidly. IASC needs a structure that will enable it to cope effectively with these and other new developments.

39.   Since the beginning of 1997, IASC has achieved impressive results by increasing the length and frequency of Board meetings from three meetings a year of three or four days each to four meetings a year of five, six or even seven days each. However, it would be difficult for volunteers to maintain this level of activity indefinitely rather than for a limited time to achieve a well-specified and valuable objective. The status quo, as it has been since the beginning of 1997 is not sustainable. The choice is between the status quo as it was before 1997 and something else.

40.   In the Working Party's view, IASC must now consider structural changes so that it can continue to meet the need for high-quality global accounting standards. If IASC fails to meet that need, other national, regional or international bodies are likely to emerge to fill the gap in response to market pressures and become de facto global or regional standard setters.

3. OBJECTIVES OF IASC

41.   The objectives of IASC as stated in its Constitution are:

(a)   to formulate and publish in the public interest accounting standards to be observed in the presentation of financial statements and to promote their worldwide acceptance and observance; and

(b)   to work generally for the improvement and harmonisation of regulations, accounting standards and procedures relating to the presentation of financial statements.

42.   In the Working Party's view, it is important to focus IASC's objectives more precisely as follows:

(a)   to develop International Accounting Standards that require high-quality, transparent and comparable information which will help participants in capital markets and others to make economic decisions; and

(b)   to promote the use of International Accounting Standards by working with national standard setters to:

(i)   bring about convergence, for listed enterprises (i.e. enterprises with publicly traded equity or debt securities) and other economically significant enterprises, between national accounting standards and International Accounting Standards; and

(ii)   encourage national, regional and international authorities to permit or require unlisted enterprises that, individually, are not economically significant to use International Accounting Standards if those Standards meet the needs of the users of the financial statements of such enterprises.

43.   The following aspects of this conclusion are discussed below:

(a)   the need for high-quality, transparent and comparable information to support economic decisions;

(b)   working with national standard setters;

(c)   convergence of standards for listed and other economically significant enterprises;

(d)   small and medium-sized enterprises (SMEs);

(e)   countries in transition and developing and newly industrialised countries; and

(f)   the public sector and not-for-profit organisations.

HIGH-QUALITY, TRANSPARENT AND COMPARABLE INFORMATION TO SUPPORT ECONOMIC DECISIONS

44.   The Working Party believes that it is vital for IASC to continue to use an agreed conceptual Framework (the Framework for the Preparation and Presentation of Financial Statements) to ensure that its standards are of high quality and require transparent and comparable information to help participants in capital markets and others to make economic decisions. The Framework may need to be revised from time to time on the basis of IASC's experience of working with it.

45.   IASC's Framework states that it is concerned with general purpose financial statements directed toward the common information needs of a wide range of users. The Framework argues that the objective of financial statements is to provide information about the financial position, performance and changes in financial position of an enterprise that is useful to a wide range of users in making economic decisions.

46.   If financial statements meet the needs of participants in the capital markets (present and potential investors and lenders), the Framework suggests they will also meet most of the needs that are common to other users of financial statements, such as employees, suppliers and other trade creditors, governments and their agencies and the public.

47.   The Working Party strongly supports the Framework's focus on information that will meet the needs of the capital markets and so also meet most of the common needs of other users.

48.   The Framework identifies four qualitative characteristics that make the information in financial statements useful to users. In summary, the information should be:

   (a)   readily understandable by users;

   (b)   relevant to their decision-making needs;

   (c)   reliable; and

   (d)   comparable with information provided by the enterprise itself in its financial statements through time and with information provided in the financial statements of different enterprises.

49.   The Framework states that information is relevant to the decision-making needs of users when it helps them to evaluate past, present or future events or confirm, or correct, their past evaluations. For example, information about the current financial position and past performance and cash flows has value to users when they evaluate the ability of an enterprise to generate cash and cash equivalents.

50.   To be reliable, the Framework argues that information must:

   (a)   represent faithfully the transactions and other events it either purports to represent or could reasonably be expected to represent;

(b) account for, and present, transactions and other events that it purports to represent in accordance with their substance and economic reality and not merely their legal form;

(c) be neutral, that is free from bias;

(d) contend with the uncertainties that inevitably surround many events and circumstances by the exercise of prudence; and

(e) be complete within the bounds of materiality and cost.

51. The Framework notes the need for a balancing, or trade-off, between the four qualitative characteristics listed in paragraph 48 above. It also recognises that the provision of relevant and reliable information may be constrained by the need for timely reporting and for a balance between costs and benefits.

52. The Working Party believes that the qualitative characteristics identified by the Framework are a sound basis for judging whether information is of high quality and will help users to make economic decisions.

53. When IASC completes the core standards, it is likely that IASC will have to give some attention to issues such as:

(a) a review of IASC's Framework for the Preparation and Presentation of Financial Statements;

(b) care, maintenance and possible amendment of existing IASC standards, particularly those approved before the Framework was developed; and

(c) industry standards. IASC has issued a standard, IAS 30, for banks and similar financial institutions, and has started projects on agriculture, insurance and the extractive industries (mining, oil and gas). In due course, IASC may consider projects on other industries.

54. In creating International Accounting Standards, IASC has generally adopted one or more accounting treatments that already existed at the national level in some countries, perhaps with some modifications in certain cases. In recent years, IASC has taken on a more innovatory role in certain projects. For example, in March 1997, IASC's Steering Committee on Financial Instruments published proposals for dealing with financial assets and financial liabilities and those proposals went beyond any requirements or proposals that existed at a national level.

55. The development of innovative solutions will inevitably require greater resources, and may demand more significant changes to IASC's working methods, than was the case when IASC saw its main role as being to choose between existing national treatments. The Working Party believes that IASC should, in close partnership with national standard setters and other constituents, play an innovatory role in areas of increasing importance to IASC's constituents. Such areas may include:

(a) the growing use of new technology, such as the Internet and CD-ROMs, to deliver financial information in new ways. This may create a need for different or additional types of financial reporting standards;

(b)   emerging issues such as environmental reporting and accounting for human resources and intellectual capital; and

(c)   broader aspects of financial and other performance reporting outside the traditional financial statements, for example:

(i)   financial reporting in a Management Discussion and Analysis ("MD&A"), Directors' Report, or similar document;

(ii)   prospective financial information; and

(iii)   non-financial measures of performance.

WORKING WITH NATIONAL STANDARD SETTERS

56.   The Working Party believes that IASC should, in developing International Accounting Standards, and in promoting their use, work closely with national standard setters to reach mutual agreement on what the highest quality result is. The aim is to ensure that national accounting standards and International Accounting Standards converge around high-quality solutions. The Working Party believes that IASC should work for convergence by:

(a)   continuing to develop International Accounting Standards that build on the best features of existing and newly developed national standards. For topics where national standards do not yet exist, or are still evolving, IASC will need to work with national standard setters to develop high-quality requirements that lead to transparency and comparability;

(b)   acting as a catalyst for, or initiator of, national developments in standard setting; and

(c)   keeping existing International Accounting Standards under review in the light of the latest thinking at national and international levels. In some cases, this review may lead to the conclusion that a national standard provides greater transparency or comparability than an existing International Accounting Standard. In such cases, IASC will need to consider amending its existing Standard.

CONVERGENCE OF STANDARDS FOR LISTED AND OTHER ECONOMICALLY SIGNIFICANT ENTERPRISES

57.   Over the last few years, IASC has put emphasis on developing core standards that are suitable for cross-border capital raising and listing purposes. However, the Working Party believes that IASC should not restrict itself to developing standards for cross-border listings. Instead, IASC should develop standards for all listed and other economically significant enterprises, because:

(a)   although certain countries may prefer for some time to require some enterprises (for example, those with cross-border listings) to use International Accounting Standards and to let other enterprises use a separate set of domestic standards, it will become increasingly difficult to justify the co-existence of two bodies of standards in the same country; and

(b)   rapid globalisation means that many enterprises have foreign providers of capital or other foreign users of their financial statements, even if the securities of those enterprises are not traded on foreign markets.

58.   The Working Party believes that IASC should, in partnership with national standard setters, make every effort to accelerate convergence between national accounting standards and International Accounting Standards around solutions requiring listed and other economically significant enterprises in all countries to report high-quality, transparent and comparable information that will help participants in capital markets and others to make economic decisions. Although IASC and national standard setters have worked together successfully and narrowed the differences between accounting standards and procedures in different countries, the remaining differences cannot be eliminated overnight. In the Working Party's view:

(a)   IASC's short-term aim should be for national accounting standards and International Accounting Standards to converge around high-quality solutions; and

(b)   IASC's aim in the longer term should be global uniformity - a single set of high-quality accounting standards for all listed and other economically significant business enterprises around the world. It is not possible to forecast how long this will take, as different countries are likely to converge with uniform global standards at different rates.

SMALL AND MEDIUM-SIZED ENTERPRISES (SMEs)

59.   The Preface to International Accounting Standards and the Framework state that International Accounting Standards apply to the financial statements of all commercial, industrial and business reporting enterprises, in both the public and private sectors. However, IASC's top priority since 1995 has been to complete the package of "core" standards required by IOSCO for cross-border listings. Therefore, some people feel IASC is developing standards that are suitable only for large multinational enterprises and enterprises with cross-border listings.

60.   Some have proposed that IASC should create exemptions for small and medium sized enterprises (SMEs), such as the exemptions found in the European Accounting Directives, or for non-listed enterprises. It is indeed possible that cost-benefit factors (acknowledged by the Framework as a constraint) may sometimes suggest one answer to an issue for large enterprises and a different answer for SMEs. Relevant factors for SMEs may include:

(a)   a narrower range of users; and

(b)   the fact that many SMEs are more constrained by tax and distribution rules as they are not part of a group and thus do not issue consolidated financial statements.

61.   Currently, as the Board debates each proposed Standard, it considers whether different requirements (for example, simpler recognition and measurement rules or disclosure exemptions) are needed for particular classes of enterprises. In most cases, the Board has felt that its Standards should apply to all enterprises, but there are a few exceptions:

(a)   IAS 14, Segment Reporting, and IAS 33, Earnings Per Share, and the proposals in E62, Financial Instruments: Recognition and Measurement, apply only to enterprises with publicly traded equity or debt securities. In practice, this is also the case for IAS 34, Interim Financial Reporting, which applies if an enterprise is required or elects to publish an interim financial report under International Accounting Standards; and

(b)   IAS 15, Information Reflecting the Effects of Changing Prices, applied originally only to listed and other economically significant enterprises. (Since 1989, IAS 15 has been non-mandatory for all enterprises.)

62.   The Working Party believes that:

(a)   regulators and standard setters in each country should decide, in the light of local circumstances:

(i)   whether International Accounting Standards are appropriate for SMEs in that country;

(ii)   how SMEs should be defined in that country; and

(iii)   what accounting standards should be used by SMEs in that country; and

(b)   it is likely that many countries will choose to bring accounting standards for SMEs into line with International Accounting Standards. Therefore, IASC must be prepared to re-evaluate the entire package of International Accounting Standards and consider whether they are appropriate for SMEs.

ECONOMIES IN TRANSITION AND DEVELOPING AND NEWLY INDUSTRIALISED COUNTRIES

63.   Countries in transition to a market economy and developing and newly industrialised countries benefit from IASC's work because they do not need to devote their own scarce resources to developing financial reporting standards. However, some argue that IASC does not pay enough attention to the needs of users and preparers in these countries. Some of these countries are already represented on the Board and one current IASC project - Agriculture - is intended partly to help such countries.

64.   As IASC's resources are limited, IASC could not devote enough time and effort to succeed with the IOSCO programme and at the same time carry out a comprehensive review to ensure that its Standards meet the needs of countries in transition and developing countries. Instead, IASC chose a more realistic strategy - first concentrate on the IOSCO programme and then see whether more needs to be done for developing countries. Also, the growing acceptance of International Accounting Standards in industrialised countries is likely to increase IASC's credibility in developing countries.

65.   For the reasons given earlier, the Working Party's belief is that, in time, all listed and other economically significant enterprises (including those in countries in transition and developing countries) should apply International Accounting Standards. Also, many developing countries have decided that International Accounting Standards are useful for SMEs.

66. In April 1998, the IASC Board approved a proposal for a project to investigate the accounting needs of economies in transition and developing and newly industrialised countries. The Working Party supports IASC's continuing investigations in this area.

PUBLIC SECTOR AND NOT-FOR-PROFIT ORGANISATIONS

67. IASC's Constitution does not limit IASC's objectives to financial reporting by business enterprises. However, to date, IASC has focused on financial reporting by business enterprises and has not dealt with:

    (a)   financial reporting in the public sector; and

    (b)   financial reporting by not-for-profit organisations, such as charities.

68. Currently, accounting and auditing standards for the public sector are being developed by the Public Sector Committee of IFAC, the International Federation of Accountants. The Public Sector Committee uses International Accounting Standards as a basis in developing its own accounting standards.

69. Some countries, notably Australia and New Zealand, are establishing common standards for both private and public sectors. The standard setters in those countries might find it more convenient if IASC were to take over responsibility for financial reporting in the public sector from IFAC. The Working Party acknowledges that this may be desirable in the longer term but notes the need to make the most effective use of IASC's limited resources. For this reason, the Working Party believes that IASC should continue to concentrate on business enterprises in the private sector for the time being and maintain a close dialogue with the Public Sector Committee.

70. The Working Party believes that IASC should not focus on financial reporting by not-for-profit organisations at this stage. However, it is likely to become important for IASC to address this topic at some point in the future.

4. IASC'S STRUCTURE AND DUE PROCESS TODAY

DESCRIPTION OF THE CURRENT STRUCTURE

71.   The current version of IASC's Constitution was approved by the Members of IASC in 1992. Amendments to the Constitution must be discussed with the Council of IFAC and require a three-quarters majority of the IASC Board and approval by the Members of IASC as expressed by a simple majority of those voting.

72.   IASC's Constitution sets out the powers of the Members and of the IASC Board. In addition, the IASC Board has established an Advisory Council, Steering Committees, a Standing Interpretations Committee and an Executive Committee. The roles of each of these bodies, and of the IASC staff and of IFAC, are discussed below.

Member Bodies

73.   The Members of IASC are all those professional accountancy bodies that are Members of the International Federation of Accountants (IFAC). IASC currently has 143 Members in 103 countries. A meeting of the Members is held every two and a half years in conjunction with each General Assembly of IFAC.

74.   Under IASC's Constitution, the Members have no direct role in the approval of International Accounting Standards or the appointment of the IASC Board.

IASC Board

75.   Under the IASC Constitution, the Members of IASC have delegated the responsibility for all IASC's activities to the IASC Board. The Board has the power to:

(a)   co-opt up to four organisations having an interest in financial reporting on to the Board;

(b)   remove from membership of the Board any Board Member whose financial contribution is more than one year in arrears or which fails to be represented at two successive Board meetings;

(c)   publish documents relating to international accounting issues for discussion and comment provided a majority of the Board votes in favour of publication;

(d)   issue documents in the form of exposure drafts for comment (including amendments to existing standards) in the name of the International Accounting Standards Committee provided that at least two-thirds of the Board votes in favour of publication;

(e)   issue International Accounting Standards provided that at least three-quarters of the Board votes in favour of publication;

(f)   establish operating procedures so long as they are not inconsistent with the provisions of IASC's Constitution;

(g)   enter into discussions, negotiations or associations with outside bodies and generally promote the world-wide improvement and harmonisation of accounting standards; and

(h)   seek and obtain funds from Members of IASC and non-members which are interested in supporting the objectives of IASC provided that such funding is organised in such a way that it does not impair the independence, or the appearance of independence, of IASC.

76.   It follows from the powers granted to the Board that it is, at present, solely responsible for, among other things:

(a)   determining the due process used to develop International Accounting Standards;

(b)   choosing topics on its work programme and the priorities attached to those topics; and

(c)   appointing Steering Committees, the Consultative Group, the Advisory Council and the Executive Committee.

77.   The Board comprises:

(a)   thirteen country Members, appointed by the Council of IFAC after seeking the advice of the outgoing Board; and

(b)   up to four co-opted Members, appointed by the Board itself.

78.   The thirteen country Members represent Members of IASC. To widen the membership of the Board, the Council of IFAC has appointed more than one country to share certain seats. Under the Constitution, the thirteen country Members are appointed by the Council of IFAC for up to five years, although recent appointments have been for two and a half years. Board Members may be re-appointed without limit.

79.   Under Mutual Commitments agreed between IFAC and IASC, the Council of IFAC nominates to the IASC Board, after seeking the advice of the outgoing Board:

(a)   at least nine of the most significant countries in terms of the status and development of the accountancy profession or that are of significant importance to international commerce and trade; and

(b)   preferably, not less than three developing countries.

The Council of IFAC must satisfy itself that the nominees have standards and resources which would enable them to contribute to the work of the Board and are willing on the invitation of the Board to nominate persons to carry out assignments or to join Working Parties or groups constituted to undertake tasks allotted by the Board.

80.   The co-opted Members are organisations with an interest in financial reporting. The terms of the co-opted Board Members are determined by the Board itself, with no upper limit.

81.   For the two and a half year term ending 30 June 2000, the Board Members are:

Country Members (date of joining the Board in parentheses)

- Australia (1973)
- Canada (1973)
- France (1973)
- Germany (1973)
- India (1993) with Sri Lanka (1995)
- Japan (1973)
- Malaysia (1995)
- Mexico (1973-1988, re-appointed 1995)
- Netherlands (1973)
- Nordic Federation of Public Accountants (1988)
- South Africa (1978) with Zimbabwe (1995)
- United Kingdom (1973)
- United States of America (1973)

Co-opted Members (one seat vacant)

- International Council of Investment Associations (1986)
- Federation of Swiss Industrial Holding Companies (1995)
- IAFEI - International Association of Financial Executives Institutes (1996)

82.   Each Board Member has one vote. Decisions are taken on a simple majority of the Board, except that a positive vote by two-thirds of all Board Members is required to approve an Exposure Draft and a positive vote by three-quarters of all Board Members is required to approve an International Accounting Standard, or, subject to the ratification of IASC's Members, to approve changes to the Constitution.

83.   Each Board Member may nominate up to two representatives and a technical adviser to attend Board meetings. Neither the Board nor IASC can compel Board Members to nominate particular individuals, or individuals with particular characteristics. However, the Board encourages each Board Member to include in its delegation at least one person working in business and one person who is directly involved in the work of the national standard setting body.

84.   The IASC Constitution states that Board Representatives shall not regard themselves as representing sectional interests but shall be guided by the need to act in the public interest.

85.   The President of IFAC, or his designate, accompanied by not more than one technical adviser, is entitled to attend IASC Board meetings and may speak but not vote. Also, at the invitation of the Board, representatives of the following currently attend Board meetings as observers:
- European Commission
- United States Financial Accounting Standards Board (FASB)
- International Organization of Securities Commissions (IOSCO)
- Public Sector Committee of IFAC
- China

86. The IASC Chairman is elected by the Board for a non-renewable term of two-and-a-half years. The Board has applied an informal policy that the Chairmanship should rotate between different regions. For continuity, the Board also normally appoints a Deputy Chairman who then takes up the Chairmanship for the next term.

87. The Board agreed in November 1997 to appoint two Vice-Chairmen for the next term, instead of a Deputy Chairman. The main reasons for this are to:

    (a) avoid the need to identify a Chairman-elect at a time when, because of the current strategy review, the Chairman's role is under review; and

    (b) spread the increasing burden of speaking commitments and other promotional and representational duties more widely.

88. The IASC Board used to meet three times a year for three or four days at a time. In 1996 the Board agreed to accelerate its work programme under an agreement with IOSCO. As a result, the Board now meets four times a year for five or six days at a time. This imposes heavy demands on the Board and it would be difficult for a Board made up of volunteers to continue meeting so often once the IOSCO work programme is completed.

Advisory Council

89. In 1995, IASC established an Advisory Council to promote generally the acceptability of International Accounting Standards and enhance the credibility of IASC's work by, among other things:

    (a) reviewing and commenting on the Board's strategy and plans so as to satisfy itself that the needs of IASC's constituencies are being met;

    (b) preparing an annual report on the effectiveness of the Board in achieving its objectives and in carrying out its due process;

    (c) promoting participation in, and acceptance of, the work of IASC by the accountancy profession, the business community, the users of financial statements and other interested parties;

    (d) seeking and obtaining funding for IASC's work in a way that does not impair IASC's independence; and

    (e) reviewing IASC's budget and financial statements.

90. Among other things, the Advisory Council aims to ensure that the independence and objectivity of the Board in making technical decisions on proposed International Accounting Standards are not impaired. The Advisory Council does not participate in, nor seek to influence, those decisions.

91. The members of the Advisory Council are outstanding individuals in senior positions from the accountancy profession, business and other users of financial statements from different backgrounds. The Advisory Council does not include representatives of national standard setters. The Chairman, Deputy-Chairman and Secretary-General of IASC are invited to, and expected to attend, all meetings of the Advisory Council but the Council is free to meet without them.

Steering Committees

92.   For its technical projects, the Board normally appoints a Steering Committee to:

       (a)   direct the preliminary research carried out by the staff;

       (b)   submit a Point Outline to the Board, in order to clarify the scope of the project;

       (c)   in the light of the Board's comments on the Point Outline, prepare and publish a Draft Statement of Principles;

       (d)   in the light of public comments on the Draft Statement of Principles, prepare and submit a Statement of Principles to the Board;

       (e)   based on the Statement of Principles approved by the Board, prepare and submit a draft Exposure Draft to the Board; and

       (f)   in the light of public comments on the Exposure Draft, prepare and submit a draft of the final International Accounting Standard to the Board.

For certain projects, the Board allows Steering Committees to omit one or more of stages (b), (c) and (d).

93.   Steering Committees are chaired by a Board Representative and usually have around six to eight members. Most Steering Committee members are neither Board Representatives nor members of their national standard setter. The candidates for membership of a Steering Committee may be nominated by Members of IASC, other organisations that are represented on the Board or the Consultative Group and other organisations that are expert in the particular topic. In appointing Steering Committees, the Board seeks both a geographical balance and a mix of accountants in public practice, preparers and users. The Board also aims to ensure that the Steering Committee has sufficient specialist knowledge of the topic.

94.   The Constitution states that members of Steering Committees shall not regard themselves as representing sectional interests but shall be guided by the need to act in the public interest.

95.   The Board's current policy is to ask IOSCO to nominate an observer to attend each Steering Committee in which IOSCO has a special interest.

Standing Interpretations Committee

96.   In 1997, the IASC Board formed a Standing Interpretations Committee (SIC) to consider, on a timely basis, accounting issues that are likely to receive divergent or unacceptable treatment in the absence of authoritative guidance. Its review is within the context of existing International Accounting Standards and the IASC Framework. In developing interpretations, the SIC consults similar national committees which have been nominated for the purpose by Member Bodies.

97.   The SIC deals with issues of reasonably widespread importance, and not issues of concern to only a small set of enterprises. The interpretations cover both:

  (a)   mature issues (the potential for unsatisfactory practice within the scope of existing International Accounting Standards); and

  (b)   emerging issues (new topics relating to an existing International Accounting Standard but not considered when the standard was developed).

98.   The SIC has twelve voting members from various countries, including individuals from the accountancy profession, preparer groups and user groups. Some current members of the SIC are members of similar national bodies. IOSCO and the European Commission are non-voting observers. Because of the required time commitment, only two current members of the SIC are also Board Representatives. To ensure adequate liaison with the Board, two Board Representatives attend SIC meetings as non-voting Board Liaison Members.

99.   The SIC publishes a draft interpretation, if no more than three of its voting members have voted against the draft. The public comment period for draft interpretations is two months. After considering comments received, the SIC amends the draft as it considers necessary. If no more than three of the SIC's voting members have voted against the final interpretation, the SIC asks the Board to approve the interpretation for formal publication; as for International Accounting Standards, this requires three-quarters of the Board to vote in favour.

Consultative Group

100.   In 1981, the IASC Board established an international Consultative Group that includes representatives of international organisations of preparers and users of financial statements, stock exchanges, regulators, trade unions, lawyers, valuers and other professions and academics. The group also includes representatives or observers from development agencies, standard setters and intergovernmental organisations.

| **Current Members of the Consultative Group** |
| European Commission |
| Fédération Internationale des Bourses de Valeurs (FIBV) |
| Financial Accounting Standards Board (FASB) |
| International Actuarial Association (IAA) |
| International Association for Accounting Education and Research (IAAER) |
| International Association of Insurance Supervisors (IAIS) |
| International Banking Associations |
| International Bar Association (IBA) |
| International Chamber of Commerce (ICC) |
| International Confederation of Free Trade Unions (ICFTU), and World Confederation of Labour |
| International Finance Corporation (IFC) |
| International Valuation Standards Committee (IVSC) |
| The World Bank |
| Organisation for Economic Co-operation and Development (OECD)* |
| United Nations Division on Transnational Corporations and Investment* |
| *Observers* |

101. The Consultative Group advises the Board on technical issues in specific IASC projects, on IASC's plans and priorities as set out in the work programme, on the likely acceptability of IASC's standards and on IASC's strategy. This group plays a helpful part in IASC's due process for the setting of International Accounting Standards and in gaining acceptance for the resulting standards.

102. The Consultative Group used to meet the full Board twice a year, for one day at a time. With the increasing numbers of participants, these meetings became less productive and the Consultative Group now meets selected Board Representatives, once a year for two days at a time.

Executive Committee

103. Management of administrative matters is in the hands of an Executive Committee appointed by the Board, headed by the Chairman of IASC and including the Vice-Chairmen and a number of other Board Representatives. The Executive Committee gives the Board a report on its discussions.

IASC Staff

104. The Board is supported by a small staff based in London, headed by a Secretary-General. The staff currently comprises:

   (a)   the Secretary-General (from the UK);

   (b)   a Technical Director (from Germany), from four to six other full-time (or almost full-time) technical staff and one part-time project manager. Current and recent past technical staff have been from Canada, France, Germany, Malaysia, New Zealand, South Africa, the UK and the USA. The technical staff are generally on secondments for one to two years, although some are employed on a longer-term basis; and

   (c)   a Commercial Director and nine other support staff.

105. Two recent IASC projects have been carried out jointly with national standard setters who have supplied project managers at no cost to IASC (other than direct travel costs).

The role of IFAC

106. The accountancy profession plays a major part in supporting and funding the work of IASC. Professional accountancy bodies took the lead in establishing IASC because of the accountancy profession's important role at that time in the setting of national accounting standards in many countries. The support of the national and accountancy bodies and IFAC has contributed greatly to the acceptance of International Accounting Standards.

107. IASC's relationship with IFAC is set out in Mutual Commitments signed in 1982. In summary:

   (a)   all Members of IFAC are automatically also Members of IASC;

(b)   after seeking the advice of the outgoing Board, the Council of IFAC nominates the thirteen country Members of the IASC Board (see paragraphs 78 and 79 for further details);

(c)   the IASC Board is required to discuss with the Council of IFAC any proposed changes to the constitution of IASC. However, IFAC or IASC may amend their respective constitutions without the approval of the other body provided that such amendment is not in conflict with the substance of the Mutual Commitments (Amendments to IASC's Constitution require a three-quarters majority of the IASC Board and approval by the Members of IASC as expressed by a simple majority of those voting);

(d)   the President of IFAC or his designate is entitled to attend, and speak at, IASC Board meetings and the IASC Chairman may attend, and speak at, meetings of the Council of IFAC;

(e)   IFAC recognises IASC as the sole body having responsibility and authority to issue, in its own name, pronouncements on international accounting standards with full authority in so doing to negotiate and associate with outside bodies and to promote the worldwide acceptance and observance of those standards. IFAC shall not appoint or support any other body for this purpose and shall not itself formulate or consider or publish any other such standards but shall support the standards promulgated by IASC and shall require its Members to support the work of IASC by publishing in their respective countries every International Accounting Standard approved for issue by the Board of IASC and by using their best endeavours:

  (i)   to ensure that published financial statements comply with International Accounting Standards in all material respects and disclose the fact of such compliance;

  (ii)   to persuade governments and standard-setting bodies that published financial statements should comply with International Accounting Standards in all material respects;

  (iii)   to persuade authorities controlling securities markets and the industrial and business community that published financial statements should comply with International Accounting Standards in all material respects and disclose the fact of such compliance;

  (iv)   to ensure that the auditors satisfy themselves that the financial statements comply with International Accounting Standards in all material respects; and

  (v)   to foster acceptance and observance of International Accounting Standards internationally;

(f)   IFAC contributes one ninth of the budgeted net expenditure that the Board determines should be borne by Board members. Also, IFAC currently reimburses the cost of one Board seat. This subsidy is shared equally by India, Sri Lanka and Zimbabwe; and

(g) changes to the Mutual Commitments require both the approval of the Council of IFAC and three-quarters of the total of the votes of the Board of IASC.

DUE PROCESS

108. In the absence of specific provisions in the Constitution, it is the responsibility of the Board to establish the due process for developing standards. IASC's due process is designed to ensure that International Accounting Standards are of high quality and acceptable to the users and preparers of financial statements. The current due process is as follows:

(a) the Board sets up a Steering Committee;

(b) the Steering Committee identifies and reviews all the accounting issues associated with the topic. The Steering Committee considers the application of IASC's Framework for the Preparation and Presentation of Financial Statements to those accounting issues. The Steering Committee also studies national and regional accounting requirements and practice, including the different accounting treatments that may be appropriate in different circumstances. Having considered the issues involved, the Steering Committee may submit a Point Outline to the Board, in order to clarify the scope of the project;

(c) after receiving comments from the Board on the Point Outline, if any, the Steering Committee normally prepares and publishes a Draft Statement of Principles or other discussion document. The purpose of this Statement is to set out the underlying accounting principles that will form the basis for the preparation of an Exposure Draft. It also describes the alternative solutions considered and the reasons for recommending their acceptance or rejection. Board approval is not required for the Draft Statement of Principles. Comments are invited from all interested parties during the exposure period, usually around three months. The Board may instruct the Steering Committee to prepare an Exposure Draft without first publishing a Draft Statement of Principles;

(d) the Steering Committee reviews the comments on the Draft Statement of Principles and normally agrees a final Statement of Principles, which is submitted to the Board for approval and used as the basis for preparing an Exposure Draft of a proposed International Accounting Standard. The final Statement of Principles is available to the public on request, but is not formally published;

(e) the Steering Committee prepares a draft Exposure Draft for approval by the Board. After revision, and with the approval of at least two-thirds of the Board, the Exposure Draft is published. Comments are invited from all interested parties during the exposure period, a minimum of one month and usually at least three months; and

(f) the Steering Committee reviews the comments and prepares a draft International Accounting Standard for review by the Board. After revision, and with the approval of at least three-quarters of the Board, the standard is published.

109. Neither Steering Committee meetings nor Board meetings are open to the public. However, the Board agreed in November 1998 that Board meetings should be open to the public from 1999.

110. During this process, the Board may decide that the needs of the subject under consideration warrant additional consultation or would be better served by issuing a Discussion Paper for comment. Under the IASC Constitution, the Board has the power to publish documents relating to international accounting issues for discussion and comment provided that a majority of the Board votes in favour. In some cases, Steering Committees or the staff have issued Discussion Papers or Issues Papers without formal Board approval.

5. IMPROVING IASC'S STRUCTURE AND DUE PROCESS

111. This section considers how IASC's structure and due process may need to be adapted to respond to the new challenges identified earlier in this Discussion Paper.

EVALUATION OF THE CURRENT STRUCTURE

112. The current structure of IASC has significant strengths:

    (a) IASC has produced high-quality standards that command international support, without unnecessary delay, generally by using existing national standards as a starting point;

    (b) the geographical spread of Board membership, and the requirement that a final standard must achieve a positive vote from three-quarters of the Board as currently constituted mean that IASC must persuade a reasonably broad constituency that its proposals are appropriate - an important consideration for an organisation that cannot compel countries or individual enterprises to adopt its standards. At the same time, the required majority is not so high that progress is blocked;

    (c) most Board delegations are currently made up of three individuals (two Board Representatives and one Technical Adviser). This permits a functional mix (preparers, auditors, standard setters, financial analysts, academics and others) from most countries on the Board and gives the Board the broad perspective that comes from a diversity of backgrounds;

    (d) the part-time status of Board Representatives and technical advisers enables them to stay in touch with their constituents and to retain up-to-date experience of accounting practice in their countries;

    (e) continuity of Board membership (both delegations and their individual representatives) speeds progress, promotes consistency and builds an atmosphere of collegiality and trust which is very important;

    (f) the involvement of a wide range of people in IASC's process, through both the Board itself and Steering Committees, plays an important promotional and educational role for IASC; and

    (g) IASC functions at remarkably low direct cost.

113. IASC has achieved a great deal with the current structure. It has developed high-quality and credible standards. Its standards are widely accepted by the international capital markets. A growing number of countries are either adopting International Accounting Standards as their own standards (in some cases, with relatively minor modifications) or drastically reducing provisions in their own standards that conflict with International Accounting Standards.

114. Despite the strengths of IASC's current structure, the changes in IASC's environment mean that structural changes are needed so that IASC can anticipate the new challenges facing it and meet those challenges effectively. The Working Party has identified the following key issues that must be addressed:

(a)   partnership with national standard setters - IASC should enter into a partnership with national standard setters so that IASC can work together with them to accelerate convergence between national standards and International Accounting Standards around solutions requiring high-quality, transparent and comparable information that will help participants in capital markets and others to make economic decisions;

(b)   wider participation in the IASC Board - a wider group of countries and organisations should take part in the IASC Board, without diluting the quality of the Board's work.

(c)   appointment - the process for appointments to the IASC Board and key IASC committees should be the responsibility of a variety of constituencies, while ensuring that those appointed are competent, independent and objective.

The Working Party also believes that changes are needed to IASC's due process so that it can cope effectively with the new challenges before it. The Working Party's proposals for improving IASC's due process are set out in paragraphs 201-214.

Partnership with National Standard Setters

115.   National standard setters have been a major factor in IASC's success. They have:

(a)   helped to generate the diversity of ideas that is needed to develop the innovative solutions required in today's rapidly changing environment;

(b)   played an important role in identifying emerging issues or problems with existing standards on a timely basis;

(c)   facilitated the flow of information between their domestic constituents and IASC; and

(d)   contributed generous human and technical resources to IASC.

116.   The Working Party considers that the continued existence of strong and autonomous national standard setters will be an important ingredient in IASC's future success. The Working Party also recognises that many countries have regulations that require their national standard setters to maintain their autonomy. In addition, national standard setters will need to deal with issues that are important locally but not important enough to require priority treatment internationally.

117.   An increasingly important challenge for IASC will be to work with national standard setters to bring about convergence between national accounting standards and International Accounting Standards around solutions requiring listed enterprises (i.e. enterprises with publicly traded equity or debt securities) and other economically significant enterprises to report high-quality, transparent and comparable information that will help participants in capital markets and others to make economic decisions. The standards of many countries are already converging with International Accounting Standards. However, trends such as globalisation and the increasing pace of business and financial change have made this task more urgent. The Working Party believes that IASC and national standard setters need to find new ways of working together to minimise unnecessary delays in reaching consensus and implementing the results of that consensus.

118. IASC already works informally with national standard setters. For example, many Board Members include in their delegations at least one person who is involved in the work of the national standard setter. However, a closer and more formal partnership between IASC and national standard setters would have important benefits:

    (a) national standard setters and IASC would find it easier to co-ordinate their work programmes with each other. This would reduce the risk that different standard setters will address the same issue at different times and reach different solutions to the same issue;

    (b) national standard setters would feel that they have some "ownership" of the standards that emerge from the IASC process. This would increase the acceptability of IASC's standards to national standard setters and their constituents;

    (c) national standard setters would be more likely than before to publish Exposure Drafts that are identical, or very similar, to IASC Exposure Drafts, to complete consultation with their own constituents before IASC needs to finalise its own standard and to play a full part in the IASC process. In some cases they may consider that they have compelling national reasons for maintaining or developing differences from International Accounting Standards. However, a close partnership between IASC and the national standard setters should mean that such differences become increasingly rare; and

    (d) assistance from national standard setters in preparing Exposure drafts and Standards would greatly augment IASC's resources and result in more efficient use of the limited resources available around the world for standard setting.

119. Given the Working Party's view that national standard setters should have a more formal role in IASC, it seems natural to review the role of Steering Committees.

120. Steering Committees are relatively small groups and, despite the best efforts of the Board to secure a balanced membership, their composition is somewhat haphazard. This means that a relatively small change in the membership of a Steering Committee may have a large impact on its recommendations. Also, Steering Committees are made up of volunteers. Those volunteers may lack the time and the support needed to consider complex technical issues in sufficient depth and to understand how decisions in their projects interact with other current projects. These difficulties could be resolved by involving national standard setters more directly in preparing Exposure Drafts and Standards, a task that is currently done by Steering Committees.

121. The Board itself is too large to take over the work currently done by Steering Committees in preparing the detailed content of Standards. The Board comprises sixteen members, each normally represented by three individuals (two Board Representatives and one Technical Adviser). Together with observers, occasional guests and the staff, there are now usually over 70 people at the Board table. This suggests that the detailed preparation of standards should continue to be the responsibility of a smaller group than the Board. The Working Party believes that national standard setters should be closely involved in this smaller group.

Wider Participation in the IASC Board

122.   The Working Party believes that IASC should widen the composition of the Board, for the following reasons:

    (a)   IASC has achieved much greater importance and higher profile in recent years. Also, its old role as a harmoniser is evolving into a new role as an innovator. These factors mean that many more countries and organisations want a voice at the Board table; and

    (b)   developing countries and countries in transition have limited representation at the Board table (for example, China is only an observer and the countries of the former Soviet Union, Central and Eastern Europe and South America have no representation on the Board). Therefore, there is a risk that the Board will not take sufficient account of their needs and views.

Appointment

123.   The Working Party believes that IASC needs to amend the procedure for appointing organisations and individuals to its decision-making bodies, for the following reasons:

    (a)   appointments to the country seats on the IASC Board are in the hands of the accounting profession (through IFAC). Therefore, preparers, users and others feel that they are under-represented and that the Board is dominated by the accountancy profession;

    (b)   Board Members choose the individuals who will serve as their Board Representatives and Technical Advisors. Thus, there is no guarantee of a proper balance in the Board as a whole of individuals from public accounting, the business community and other users of financial statements as well as individuals who are directly involved in the work of the national standard setters; and

    (c)   a key responsibility of the Advisory Council is to monitor the Board. However, the Advisory Council may appear to lack objectivity because it is appointed by, and reports to, the Board itself.

A POSSIBLE FUTURE STRUCTURE FOR IASC

124.   The Working Party's proposals are set out in paragraphs 125-200 below.

125.   The Working Party's proposals address the key issues identified in paragraph 114 by the following changes:

    (a)   a partnership with national standard setters:

        (i)   Steering Committees would be replaced by a Standards Development Committee, on which national standard setters would play a major role in developing International Accounting Standards (see paragraphs 126-136 for its membership and paragraphs 154-159 for its responsibilities). The Standards Development Committee would also be responsible for approving the publication of final SIC Interpretations prepared by the Standing Interpretations Committee; and

(ii)   the Standards Development Committee would be supported by a Standards Development Advisory Committee, which would act as a channel of communication with those national standard setters who are unable to participate directly in the Standards Development Committee because of its limited size (see paragraphs 160-163);

(b)   wider participation in the IASC Board - the Board would have a wider membership than at present (see paragraphs 137-146 for its membership and paragraphs 164-178 for its responsibilities). The Board would still be responsible for the final approval of International Accounting Standards and Exposure Drafts; and

(c)   appointment - the Advisory Council would be replaced by Trustees (see paragraphs 147-153 for their membership and paragraphs 179-183 for their responsibilities). Among other things, the Trustees would appoint members of the Standards Development Committee, the Board and the Standing Interpretations Committee. The Trustees would also have responsibility for monitoring IASC's effectiveness and for finance.

Paragraphs 184-200 deal with other aspects of the Working Party's proposals for the structure of IASC. Paragraphs 201-214 cover the Working Party's recommendations for improving IASC's due process.

Standards Development Committee - Membership

126.   The Working Party proposes that Steering Committees should be replaced by a single Standards Development Committee to work on all IASC projects. The Standards Development Committee would prepare drafts of Exposure Drafts and International Accounting Standards for submission to the Board.

127.   To allow for effective and efficient decision-making and ensure sufficient diversity of backgrounds, the Standards Development Committee should have 11 members, appointed by the Trustees:

(a)   a full-time chairman;

(b)   six to eight individuals, each nominated by a national standard setter with the technical, human and financial resources to make a significant contribution to IASC's work. The individuals should be voting members of the national standard setter that nominated them; and

(c)   two to four members selected from other groups, such as preparers, users, accountants in public practice and academics.

128.   Criteria for membership of the Standards Development Committee should include the following:

(a)   prospective members should be people of proven technical competence in standard setting, integrity and objectivity. They should not regard themselves as representing sectional interests but should be guided by the need to act in the public interest. Therefore, they would reach their own conclusions on technical issues and not merely vote on behalf of their national standard setter or other constituency;

(b)   prospective members should accept a commitment to use IASC's Framework for the Preparation and Presentation of Financial Statements as the basis for developing Standards that require high-quality, transparent and comparable information which will help a wide range of users (including participants in the capital markets) to make economic decisions. Revisions to the Framework should go through the same due process as a new Standard;

(c)   prospective members should show, for example, by previous participation in IASC projects and by submitting comment letters on IASC proposals, that they can make an active contribution to IASC's work and that they will be able to attend meetings regularly.

(d)   if suitably qualified candidates are available, at least seven should be from more developed countries, for example, countries that are members of the OECD or other countries with large economies or large capital markets (see appendix 5 for current data) and at least two should be from developing countries or countries in transition to a market economy;

(e)   special consideration should be given to individuals from countries that:

        (i)   make, or are likely to make, extensive use of International Accounting Standards; or

        (ii)   have a high proportion of enterprises with foreign operations or that are involved in foreign trade; and

(f)   there should be a reasonable geographical spread of members.

129.   The Working Party believes that all members of the Standards Development Committee should devote at least half of their time to standard setting, including any time spent at their national standard setter. This would:

(a)   provide greater independence from employment and other allegiances that might affect their voting; and

(b)   increase their standard-setting expertise and the time they can give to technical issues.

130.   The Working Party believes that the Standards Development Committee will need a full-time Chairman. The Working Party believes that at least six other members of the Standards Development Committee should have a full time involvement in standard setting, including time spent at their national standard setter.

131.   Most national standard setters have mainly part-time members and would probably need to appoint a full-time member specifically to serve on the Standards Development Committee. The work of the Standards Development Committee would be of direct benefit to national standard setters and other constituencies. Therefore, the Working Party believes that national standard setters and other constituencies should normally pay:

(a)   the salaries of their own members on the Standards Development Committee and related costs, including insurance;

(b)   the costs of their travel between IASC and the national standards body; and

(c)   the costs of technical and other staff assigned by the national standard setter to assist the member. However, IASC should pay for the costs of IASC technical and other staff.

132.   Some countries may find it difficult to identify, and finance, a suitable individual to serve on the Standards Development Committee. The Trustees may need to seek a special arrangement with professional accountancy bodies in these countries to identify, and finance, a suitable individual. However, the Working Party recognises that it may be difficult to achieve such an arrangement.

133.   Certain countries or other constituencies may not be able to finance a member of the Standards Development Committee. The Trustees should have the power to direct IASC to pay for the costs of well-qualified individuals who would enhance the diversity of backgrounds in the Standards Development Committee.

134.   The Standards Development Committee would probably need to meet every one to two months. The use of video conferencing and e-mail may reduce the need for all members to travel to every meeting. However, most members should travel to most meetings, as face-to-face meetings are essential to ensure full communication and to build an atmosphere of collegiality and trust. To minimise logistical problems for members based outside Europe or North America, meetings may need to rotate.

135.   Standards Development Committee members should be appointed for a fixed term of five years. However, the expiry of the first terms should be staggered: two members should retire after each of three, four, six and seven years and three members should retire after five years. This will provide continuity when the Standards Development Committee is first set up. The terms of individual members should be renewable once at the discretion of the Trustees and another individual from the same country or organisation would be eligible for subsequent appointment.

136.   As stated in paragraph 204, the Working Party believes that the technical discussions of the Standards Development Committee should be open to the public. The Standards Development Committee would be free to invite members of the public to speak at its meetings. The Working Party leans towards the view that the Standards Development Committee should not have formal observers with a right to speak, but recognises that the question of regulatory representation may need further thought.

Board - Membership

137.   In some national standard setters, decisions are taken by a relatively small group of, perhaps between seven and thirteen, experts. In an international standard setter, it may be desirable to give more constituencies (both geographical and functional) representation in the body that has ultimate authority for approving Standards. The Working Party believes that the Board should have a wider membership than at present:

(a)   20 country seats for professional accountancy bodies (rather than thirteen as at present); and

(b)   five seats for other organisations with an interest in financial reporting (at present, four seats are reserved for such organisations and three are currently occupied). These should generally be international organisations, although exceptions should be permitted in limited cases.

138.   Criteria for membership of the Board should include the following:

    (a)   at least fourteen of the country Members should be more developed countries, for example, countries that are members of the OECD or other countries with large economies or large capital markets (see appendix 5 for current data) and at least four should be developing countries or countries in transition.

    (b)   special consideration should be given to countries that:

        (i)   make, or are likely to make, extensive use of International Accounting Standards; or

        (ii)   have a high proportion of enterprises with foreign operations or that are involved in foreign trade;

    (c)   there should be a reasonable geographical spread of Board Members;

    (d)   there should be a planned rotation in Board Membership that provides a reasonable balance between continuity and turnover; and

    (e)   Board Members should show that they can make an active contribution to the Board, for example, by previous participation in IASC projects and by submitting comment letters on IASC proposals.

139.   The IASC Constitution states that Board Representatives shall not regard themselves as representing sectional interests but shall be guided by the need to act in the public interest. To emphasise this point, the individuals appointed by Board Members should be described as Board Delegates and not Board Representatives.

140.   To keep discussions effective, each Board delegation should be represented by two Board Delegates, rather than the three (two Board Representatives and one Technical Adviser) individuals that form most present Board delegations.

141.   At present, each delegation has one vote. This means that Board delegations are sometimes forced to abstain where the members of the delegation are unable to agree among themselves. Given the current requirement for a positive vote by three quarters of the Board, an abstention is effectively the same as a vote against a Standard. This might suggest that each member of the delegation should be given an individual vote, to reduce the risk of deadlock. However, discussions among, say, 50 voting individuals would be much more cumbersome than discussions among 50 individuals representing 25 voting delegations. The Working Party recommends that IASC should retain the current practice that each delegation has one vote.

142.   Board Members should retain the power to appoint their Board Delegates, in consultation with the Trustees, who would have the power to veto the appointment of any individual Board Delegate. The Working Party believes that the Trustees should exercise this power extremely rarely and proposes that such a veto should require the agreement of nine of the twelve Trustees. The Trustees should develop and apply written criteria to ensure that:

    (a)   Board Delegates are people of technical competence, integrity and objectivity who will not regard themselves as representing sectional interests, but will be guided by the need to act in the public interest;

(b)   Board Delegates will accept a commitment to use IASC's Framework for the Preparation and Presentation of Financial Statements as the basis for developing Standards that require high-quality, transparent and comparable information which will help a wide range of users (including participants in the capital markets) to make economic decisions. Revisions to the Framework should go through the same due process as a new Standard;

(c)   the Board has sufficient diversity of membership, including accountants in public practice, accountants in industry, commerce and finance, people involved in national standard setting (particularly for those countries whose standard setter is not represented on the Standards Development Committee), users, academics and others;

(d)   Board Delegates can make an active contribution to IASC's work and will attend meetings regularly; and

(e)   there is a planned rotation of Board Delegates that provides a reasonable balance between continuity and turnover.

143.   All Members of the Standards Development Committee should attend Board meetings and have a right to speak at those meetings. However, to avoid conflicts of interest:

(a)   individuals who are members of the Standards Development Committee should not be eligible to serve as Board Delegates or to act as voting alternates to Board Delegates, although another individual from the same country should be eligible; and

(b)   similarly, where an individual is a member of the Standards Development Committee and also a member of a national standard setter, another individual from the same standard setter should not be eligible to serve as a Board Delegate or to act as a voting alternate to a Board Delegate.

Where an individual is a member of the Standards Development Committee and also a member of an organisation other than a national standard setter, another individual from the same organisation should be eligible to serve as a Board Delegate.

144.   Members of the Board should be appointed for a fixed term of two and a half years, renewable without limit at the discretion of the Trustees. Given the proposed criterion of a reasonable balance between continuity and turnover in Board Membership, there is no need to stagger the expiry of the terms.

145.   The Board would be chaired by a non-executive, part-time Chairman, devoting 50% of his or her time to IASC. IASC would provide secretarial support and a half-time salary. The Chairman of the Board would be the main spokesperson for IASC on matters of broad policy and on the acceptability of International Accounting Standards to IASC's constituents. The position would be similar in some respects to the non-executive chairman of a business enterprise.

146.   The Working Party proposes that the Trustees should have the power to appoint Observers with a right to speak, but not vote, at Board meetings. Observers would be regulators and other organisations who can make a contribution to the Board's debate but who are unable to take up a voting seat. There should be no formal limit on the number of observers, but the number should be kept relatively low to keep Board

meetings to a manageable size. The Working Party envisages that the Observers would include:

(a)   IOSCO;

(b)   the European Commission; and

(c)   IFAC and IFAC's Public Sector Committee and International Auditing Practices Committee.

Trustees - Membership

147.   At present, the accountancy profession (through IFAC) controls the appointments to the IASC Board. Because of the increasing importance of IASC's work, the Working Party believes that other constituents should have some say in appointments, although the accountancy profession (IFAC and the existing Member Bodies of IASC and IFAC) should retain a significant ongoing role.

148.   The Working Party proposes that the Advisory Council should be replaced by Trustees with powers and responsibilities assigned by a revised IASC Constitution, rather than delegated to them by the Board. These would include the responsibility for appointments.

149.   The Working Party proposes that there should be 12 Trustees, who would be unpaid except for the Chairman of the Trustees (to be paid on a part-time basis).

(a)   Six "constituency" Trustees should be appointed by various constituents, in consultation with the existing Trustees:

  •   three by the International Federation of Accountants (IFAC);

  •   three by other international organisations, such as those currently represented on the Consultative Group.

(b)   Six Trustees should represent the world "at large". The first six "at large" Trustees should be appointed by a nominating committee comprising the current Advisory Council, recent past chairmen of IASC and recent past presidents of IFAC (but excluding any individuals who will be candidates to serve as Trustees). For subsequent terms, the six "at large" Trustees should be appointed by the twelve Trustees.

150.   To guide constituents in nominating the "constituency" Trustees and to guide themselves in selecting the "at large" Trustees, the Trustees should develop written criteria, including the following:

(a)   Trustees should be people of integrity and objectivity who will be guided by the need to act in the public interest. Neither "constituency" Trustees nor "at large" Trustees should regard themselves as representing sectional interests;

(b)   Trustees should accept a commitment to maintaining IASC as an organisation that develops Standards that require high-quality, transparent and comparable information which will help a wide range of users (including participants in the capital markets) to make economic decisions;

(c) most of the twelve Trustees should be from more developed countries, for example, members of the OECD or other countries with large economies or large capital markets (see appendix 5 for current data), but it is desirable that some should be from developing countries or countries in transition to market economies;

(d) special consideration should be given to Trustees from countries that:

  (i) make, or are likely to make, extensive use of International Accounting Standards; or

  (ii) have a high proportion of enterprises with foreign operations or that are involved in foreign trade;

(e) there should be a reasonable geographical spread of Trustees;

(f) collectively, the Trustees should have sufficient diversity of membership, including people with current or recent experience in senior positions as users, preparers, accountants in public practice, academics, regulators and others; and

(g) Trustees should be able to make an active contribution to IASC's work and should attend meetings regularly.

151. The Trustees should appoint Chairman of the Trustees. The first Chairman should be designated by the nominating committee discussed above.

152. To avoid conflicts of interest, the Chairman of the Trustees should not be the same individual as the Chairman of the Board. Similarly, Trustees should not serve as members of the Standards Development Committee, as Board Delegates or as members of the Standing Interpretations Committee.

153. The Trustees would be appointed for a fixed term of five years (renewable once). The terms of the Trustees should be staggered so that they do not all retire at the same time. Thus, three of the first "constituency" Trustees and three of the first "at large" Trustees should retire after two and a half years.

Standards Development Committee - Responsibilities

154. The most important function of the Standards Development Committee will be to prepare Exposure Drafts and International Accounting Standards and submit them to the Board for approval. This should require approval by a "super-majority" of the Standards Development Committee (seven votes out of 11). The Standards Development Committee should also have responsibility for approval of SIC final Interpretations (by the same majority seven votes out of 11), as explained in paragraph 185. All other decisions should require a simple majority of those present.

155. The Standards Development Committee would have the power to add projects to, or remove them from, its work programme. Among other things, this will make it easier for IASC to co-ordinate work plans with national standard setters, which is an important factor in the partnership that IASC needs to forge with national standard setters.

156. The Working Party believes that the Standards Development Committee should have the authority, on a simple majority vote, to issue Draft Statements of Principles, as

well as Discussion Papers and similar documents without Board approval, although it should discuss key issues with the Board in advance. This is similar to the authority currently given to Steering Committees.

157. The close involvement of national standard setters would mean that many IASC projects could be carried out as joint projects with national standard setters. In the past, national standard setters have borne their own staff costs for joint projects, including the cost of time spent on developing IASC documents for Steering Committee and Board meetings and for publication. The Working Party believes that IASC should continue to seek the agreement of national standard setters to co-operate on this basis.

158. Explanation and promotion is a major time commitment for national standard setters. To limit the demands on the time of the Chairman of the Standards Development Committee, the Chairman of the Board should carry out many of the representative duties as ambassador for IASC. The Chairman and other members of the Standards Development Committee should also be expected to help in explaining and promoting the technical aspects of IASC's work. The Working Party hopes that national standard setters would also play a part in this, by publishing and explaining IASC proposals as a vital component of their own domestic standard setting programme.

159. The Standards Development Committee should work in whatever way it considers most effective and cost-efficient. It may wish to set up sub-groups, task forces or similar bodies for individual projects or to outsource detailed research or other work to national standard setters. The Standards Development Committee should seek agreements with national standard setters to draw on their resources, as well as relying on IASC's own staff. It may also need to set up sub-committees or advisory groups to advise it on such issues as:

(a) accounting in specialist industries, such as banking, insurance, agriculture and the extractive industries;

(b) the reporting needs of unlisted enterprises or other small and medium-sized enterprises (SMEs) and not-for-profit organisations;

(c) the needs of developing countries and countries in transition;

(d) real-time reporting and the delivery of financial information through new technology, such as the Internet and CD-ROMs;

(e) emerging issues such as environmental reporting and accounting for human resources and intellectual capital; and

(f) broader aspects of financial and other performance reporting outside the traditional financial statements (for example, non-financial measures of performance and historic and prospective financial information in a Management Discussion and Analysis, Directors' Report, or similar document).

Involving Other National Standard Setters - a Standards Development Advisory Committee

160. The need to limit the size of the Standards Development Committee means that it cannot include representatives from all standard setters in all countries. The inclusion of standard setters of the countries with the largest capital markets and a reasonable cross-section of other standard setters is likely to be a strong incentive for other standard setters to make use of IASC's work. Nevertheless, the Working Party believes that those other standard setters will need a formal channel of communication with the Standards Development Committee.

161. To provide this formal channel of communication, the Working Party recommends that there should be a Standards Development Advisory Committee. This should meet at least annually under the chairmanship of the Chairman of the Standards Development Committee. The purpose of these meetings should be to advise the Standards Development Committee whether its proposals are likely to be appropriate and operational in the domestic environment of the countries concerned. Membership of the Standards Development Advisory Committee should be at the invitation of the Trustees and should be open in principle to standard setters of any country not represented on the Standards Development Committee.

162. Among other things, the Standards Development Advisory Committee would provide a useful means for the Standards Development Committee to communicate with standard setters in countries in transition and developing and newly industrialised countries.

163. The Working Party believes that the meetings of the Standards Development Advisory Committee would replace the meetings of world standard setters that currently take place from time to time with IASC involvement.

Board - Responsibilities

164. The Working Party paid close attention to the question of the final authority to issue standards. In its discussions, the Working Party identified three crucial considerations:

    (a)   the need to convince users, preparers and IASC's other constituents that IASC's standards will meet their needs;

    (b)   the need to attract suitably qualified individuals to serve on the Standards Development Committee and the Board; and

    (c)   the need for the Standards Development Committee and the Board to work together closely and effectively for the public interest.

165. IASC cannot force anyone to use its Standards and so must rely on persuasion. It can persuade its constituents to use its Standards only if the Standards are of high quality and meet their needs. Also, IASC's constituents are more likely to use its Standards if they have a stake in, and play a meaningful part in, their development and participation by IASC's constituents is likely to improve the quality of the standards.

166. One way to persuade IASC's constituents to accept its due process and its standards would be to set up an autonomous body of independent full-time and highly skilled experts, with a relatively small number of members for the sake of efficiency (an independent expert model). Another route would be to create a more broadly-based group from a larger number of countries and backgrounds (a constituency model).

167. The Working Party believes that neither of these extremes would secure sufficient worldwide support from IASC's constituents, even with the improvements that the Working Party is proposing to IASC's due process. Instead, the Working Party's proposal combines elements of both models: a group of independent experts (the Standards Development Committee) and a broader group (the Board), coupled with a high-level of due process to ensure a wide range of input.

168. In developing its proposals, the Working Party was conscious of the need to attract talented and well-qualified individuals to serve on both the Standards Development Committee and the Board. It is unlikely that such individuals will make themselves available for a body that does not have genuine decision-making power.

169. It is clear that any structure that involves two bodies with genuine decision-making power can work only if the two bodies demonstrate a clear willingness to work together closely and effectively for the public interest. The Working Party believes that a constructive attitude of close and effective co-operation is a striking feature of the current Board and of IASC's Committees. Consequently, the Working Party is confident that the Standards Development Committee and the Board will achieve the close and effective relationship that will be needed. The Working Party also noted that constructive co-operation will not emerge if either the Standards Development Committee or the Board is unable to attract suitably qualified individuals.

170. With these three considerations in mind, the Working Party considered a range of different ways of specifying the respective powers of the Standards Development Committee and the Board. Among these were:

    (a) positive approval required by a majority or super-majority of the Board for all International Accounting Standards and Exposure Drafts;

    (b) the Board (or perhaps a specified majority or a specified minority of the Board) has the power to reject proposed International Accounting Standards and Exposure Drafts;

    (c) the Board (or perhaps a specified majority or a specified minority of the Board) has the power to return proposed International Accounting Standards and Exposure Drafts to the Standards Development Committee for re-consideration, but not to reject them indefinitely; and

    (d) the Standards Development Committee must consult the Board, but the Board has no power to delay or reject International Accounting Standards or Exposure Drafts.

171. Individual members of the Working Party have preferences for different points in this range. Some members of the Working Party prefer option (a) above. Other members of the Working Party prefer option (d) above. However, the Working Party believes that the precise voting arrangements are less important than the need for the Standards Development Committee and the Board to work together constructively. As

explained above, the Working Party is confident that the Standards Development Committee and the Board will achieve the close and effective relationship that will be needed and will maintain a close dialogue throughout each project.

172. The Working Party proposes that publication of a Standard or Exposure Draft should require approval by 60% of the Board (15 votes out of 25). At present, an Exposure Draft requires a positive vote by two thirds of the Board; a final Standard requires a positive vote by three quarters of the Board. The Working Party further concluded that the Chairman of the Board should be required to ensure that the Board considers and votes on all proposed Exposure Drafts and Standards submitted by the Standards Development Committee within three months of receipt or, if later, at its next meeting.

173. If the Board rejects a proposed Exposure Draft or Standard, the Board should send the document back to the Standards Development Committee for further consideration, giving public reasons for its rejection. After considering the reasons given by the Board, the Standards Development Committee may decide to:

    (a)   prepare a revised proposal and submit it to the Board for approval in the normal way; or

    (b)   resubmit its original proposal to the Board:

        (i)   if nine or more members of the Standards Development Committee have voted to resubmit the same proposal, Board approval should require a simple majority (13 votes out of 25); and

        (ii)   if seven or eight members of the Standards Development Committee have voted to resubmit the proposal, the proposal should be treated in the same way as a new proposal. In other words, Board approval should require the normal 60% majority (i.e. 15 votes out of 25).

174. The Working Party believes that the Board should not have the power to amend proposed Exposure Drafts and Standards submitted by the Standards Development Committee.

175. The Working Party believes that the proposals set out in paragraphs 172-174 will ensure reasonably widespread acceptance for IASC's work, without undue risk of paralysing the work of the Standards Development Committee. It will also give genuine decision-making power to both the Standards Development Committee and the Board.

176. The Working Party recommends that the Board should have the right to add projects to the Standards Development Committee's work plan, but should not have the right to remove projects from the work plan. The Standards Development Committee should seek regular guidance on its work plan from the Board. The Standards Development Committee should also discuss the main technical issues in all its proposals with the Board in depth at an early stage and as projects progress.

177. The Working Party considers that:

    (a)   a majority of 60% (i.e. 15 votes out of 25) should be required to consent to changes in the Constitution (see paragraph 183); and

(b) all other Board decisions should require a simple majority of those present.

178. The Board would probably need to meet three times a year.

Trustees - Responsibilities

179. The Working Party proposes that the Advisory Council should be replaced by Trustees with powers and responsibilities assigned by a revised IASC Constitution, rather than delegated to them by the Board. These powers and responsibilities would include:

(a) appointing members of the Standards Development Committee and the Standing Interpretations Committee, Board Members and the Chairmen and Vice-Chairmen of the Standards Development Committee, Board and Standing Interpretations Committee. The Trustees should draw up written criteria for this purpose;

(b) liaising with Board Members to ensure that Board Delegates are appointed who have the appropriate personal qualities to contribute to the Board and who, in aggregate, have an appropriate mix of backgrounds and experience. The Trustees would have the power to veto the appointment of any individual Board Delegate. The Working Party believes that the Trustees should exercise this power extremely rarely and proposes that such a veto should require the agreement of nine of the twelve Trustees. The Trustees should draw up written criteria for this purpose;

(c) ratifying the appointments (by the Chairman of the Standards Development Committee) of the Technical Director and Commercial Director;

(d) monitoring the ability of IASC's structure to lead to results that meet IASC's objectives;

(e) reviewing the effectiveness of the Standards Development Committee and the Board in meeting IASC's objectives;

(f) reviewing broad strategic issues and relationships with key constituents (for example, IOSCO, IFAC, the World Bank Group and national standard setters) in consultation with the Board and the Standards Development Committee;

(g) promoting IASC and its work;

(h) approving IASC's budget and monitoring the efficient use of its resources;

(i) fund-raising;

(j) publishing an annual written report on IASC's activities and the work of the Trustees and presenting a formal report to the members of IASC every two and a half years; and

(k) proposing changes to IASC's Constitution.

180. The Trustees should have the power to set up sub-committees as necessary. In particular, the Trustees should set up a Selection Sub-committee consisting of Trustees. The Selection Sub-committee would identify candidates for the Standards

Development Committee (in consultation with the Chairmen and Vice-Chairmen of the Board and Standards Development Committee and with national standard setters and other organisations who employ potential candidates), Standing Interpretations Committee, Board and "at large" Trustees.

181.   The Trustees should do nothing to impair the independence and objectivity of the Board, the Standards Development Committee or the Standing Interpretations Committee and should not participate in their technical decisions. Thus, the Trustees should not intervene in technical disputes on individual projects between the Standards Development Committee and the Board. In the unlikely event of prolonged or repeated disputes between the Standards Development Committee and the Board, the Trustees would need to consider whether IASC's structure enables IASC to meet its objectives.

182.   To avoid conflicts of interest, fund-raising should be the responsibility of the Trustees and not a responsibility of members of the Standards Development Committee and Board Delegates.

183.   Changes to the Constitution should require approval by all of the following:

(a)   60% of the Trustees (8 votes out of 12);

(b)   60% of the Board (15 votes out of 25); and

(c)   a simple majority of those members of IASC who vote on the proposed change.

Standing Interpretations Committee

184.   The Working Party believes that the Standing Interpretations Committee (SIC) should continue to exist as a separate body, because neither the Board nor the Standards Development Committee would have sufficient time to develop their own Interpretations.

185.   At present, Board approval is required for a final Interpretation. Some members of the Working Party believe that this should continue. However, a majority of the Working Party would prefer final approval by the Standards Development Committee, to minimise delays in issuing Interpretations that may be needed urgently and because they believe that the SIC's own due process makes formal approval by the Board unnecessary. They propose that this should require the same majority as a decision to submit an Exposure Draft or Standard to the Board for approval (seven votes out of 11).

186.   When the SIC submits final Interpretations to the Standards Development Committee for approval, it should also send a copy to Board Members so that they can comment to the Standards Development Committee before it approves the final Interpretation.

187.   The Working Party believes that members of the SIC should be appointed by the Trustees. To avoid delays in filling vacancies on the SIC, the Working Party recommends that the Trustees should have the power to establish a Sub-Committee for this purpose.

188.   The Working Party believes that one member of the Standards Development Committee and one Board Delegate should attend SIC meetings as observers.

189.   It is too early to assess whether any other changes are needed to the structure or procedures of the Standing Interpretations Committee (SIC), which was formed in 1997.

Consultative Group

190.   The Working Party believes that IASC should maintain the Consultative Group as a useful forum for dialogue with organisations (mainly international) that have an interest in financial reporting. The Consultative Group should meet once or twice a year with the Chairmen of the Standards Development Committee, Board and Trustees and others as appropriate. The meetings should be chaired by the Chairman of the Board. The purpose of the meetings should be for the Consultative Group to:

(a)   give feedback on IASC proposals, guidance on work plan priorities and advice on relationships with key constituencies; and

(b)   receive reports on IASC's work

Members of IASC

191.   The Working Party believes that the Members of IASC should continue to be the professional accountancy bodies that are members of IFAC and should continue to meet every two and a half years. The Members of IASC should meet under the Chairmanship of the Chairman of the Trustees to:

(a)   receive a report by the Trustees on their activities over the preceding two and a half years;

(b)   receive reports by the Chairmen of the Board and the Standards Development Committee on the activities, work programme and future strategy of the Board and the Standards Development Committee; and

(c)   ratify (by a simple majority of those voting) any changes to IASC's Constitution that have been approved by the Trustees and Board (see paragraph 183).

Executive Committee

192.   The Working Party believes that the Board will no longer need an Executive Committee. Certain issues of an administrative nature would be handled conveniently by informal discussions between the Chairmen of the Standards Development Committee, Board and Trustees. As noted in Paragraph 180, the Trustees should have the power to set up sub-committees as they see fit.

Staff

193.   As effective chief executive officer, the Chairman of the Standards Development Committee would take over the functions currently performed by the Secretary-General, except that the Chairman of the Board would carry out many of the representative duties as ambassador for IASC.

194.   Under the Working Party's proposals, technical functions are the province of the Standards Development Committee and the Board, while commercial functions (including funding, copyright, office, equipment, communications) are the province of the Trustees. The Working Party proposes that:

(a)   technical functions should be headed by a Technical Director, reporting to the Standards Development Committee; and

(b)   commercial functions should be headed by a Commercial Director, reporting through the Chairman of the Standards Development Committee to the Trustees.

The Technical Director and Commercial Director should be appointed by the Chairman of the Standards Development Committee, subject to ratification by the Trustees.

195.   To play an equal role in partnership with national standard setters, IASC needs a core of high-quality technical staff (at least eight), at a central location. Some projects would be joint projects with national standard setters and staffed predominantly by the national standard setter concerned. However, IASC's own staff would need to monitor the staff work on these projects to ensure that the output meets IASC's needs.

196.   The Technical Staff would provide technical support to the Standards Development Committee and the Board. The Working Party does not believe that these functions need to be separated. The Commercial Director would be responsible for administrative support for the Board and the Trustees.

Legal Structure

197.   IASC is not a legal entity. This is administratively inconvenient. For example, it causes practical difficulty in enforcing IASC's copyright. Also, it creates a risk, however remote, that third parties might seek to make Members of IASC, Board Members, or even individual Board Delegates, liable for acts or omissions of IASC. The Working Party recommends that the Board should consider ways of establishing IASC as a legal entity. The Working Party believes that the establishment of a separate legal entity would also be more in keeping with IASC's future role.

198.   The Working Party believes that IASC should investigate the possibility of seeking charitable or similar status in those countries where such status would assist fund-raising.

Timetable for Change

199.   A possible timetable for implementing the Working Party's proposals is set out in appendix 6. Certain aspects of the Working Party's proposals would require changes to IASC's Constitution. As explained above, constitutional changes must be discussed with the Council of IFAC and require a three-quarters majority of the IASC Board and approval by the Members of IASC as expressed by a simple majority of those voting. The next meeting of the Members of IASC is planned for May 2000.

200.   The possible timetable in Appendix 6 assumes that IASC plans for these changes as soon as possible on the assumption that the members of IASC approve the changes in May 2000. For example, the process of selecting the Trustees should begin at an early

stage, so that provisional Trustees can, on a provisional basis, begin selecting members of the Board and Standards Development Committee. The provisional appointments could then come into effect as soon as the Members of IASC have approved the revised constitution. The revised structure would then come into effect from 1 July 2000, when the term of the current Board expires. The Working Party recognises that this is a challenging timetable, which relies on the optimistic assumption that a provisional selection process can be largely completed before the necessary constitutional changes have been approved.

DUE PROCESS

201.   To safeguard IASC's legitimacy, IASC's due process must ensure that International Accounting Standards are of high quality, requiring transparent and comparable information that will help participants in capital markets and others to make economic decisions, and that its standards are acceptable to the users and preparers of financial statements. Given IASC's higher profile today, the greatly increased interest in its work and IASC's changing role, it is appropriate to seek improvement of IASC's due process.

Open Meetings or Closed Meetings?

202.   All IASC meetings are closed, although the Board agreed in November 1998 that Board meetings should be open to the public from 1999. The possible advantages of closed meetings are that:

(a)   participants may find it easier to engage in open exchanges of ideas when they do not feel that they are on public display. This may be particularly true for participants from cultures that do not encourage public dissent and for those whose mother tongue is not English;

(b)   the debates may be less politicised than in open meetings; and

(c)   open meetings may lead to delays and extra cost.

203.   The possible advantages of open meetings (a "sunshine" policy), are that they would:

(a)   lead to better standards (through more effective public scrutiny); and

(b)   increase public confidence in IASC and strengthen its legitimacy.

204.   The Working Party believes that:

(a)   all formal discussions of the Standards Development Committee, Standing Interpretations Committee and Board on technical issues should be open to the public. However, certain discussions (primarily selection, appointment and other personnel issues) would need to be held in private. Portions of the Trustees' meetings should also be open to the public, at the discretion of the Trustees;

(b)   IASC should make more use of new technology (such as the Internet, the web site, electronic observation of meetings), to overcome geographical barriers and the logistical problems in arranging for members of the public to attend open meetings of an international body;

(c)   IASC should publish in advance the agendas for each meeting of the Standards Development Committee, Standing Interpretations Committee, Board and Trustees and should publish promptly the decisions made at those meetings (IASC currently publishes the agenda for Board meetings in its quarterly newsletter, *Insight*, and on its web site. IASC also publishes Board decisions immediately after each Board meeting in *Update* and SIC decisions in *News From The SIC*); and

(d)   when IASC publishes a Standard, it should continue its recently adopted practice of publishing a Basis for Conclusions to explain publicly how it reached its conclusions and to give background information that may help users of IASC standards to apply them in practice. IASC should also publish dissentient opinions (IASC's current Constitution prohibits this).   These would be brief summaries, prepared by IASC's staff, of the reasons given by members of the Standards Development Committee and Board for voting against the Standard.

Public Hearings and Field Tests

205.   The Working Party believes that the Standards Development Committee should make use of the following, although there should be no requirement to do so for every project:

(a)   "public hearings" to discuss proposed standards (Steering Committees have occasionally held similar meetings in the past, for example, in 1995, on Segment Reporting, and in 1997, on Financial Instruments); and

(b)   field tests (both in developed countries and in emerging markets) to ensure that proposals are practical and workable.

Where practicable, public hearings and field tests should be co-ordinated with national standard setters.

Co-ordination with National Due Process

206.   An important objective of the Working Party's model is closer co-ordination between IASC's due process and the due process of national standard setters, who will necessarily remain autonomous.   The Working Party recognises that many national standard setters will not give up their own due process, nor can they give an irrevocable undertaking that they will tie themselves completely on every project to IASC's due process. However, the Working Party believes that IASC should aim to integrate IASC's due process more closely with national due process.   This is something that will probably not happen overnight but will occur gradually as the relationship between IASC and national standard setters evolves.   The Working Party's desired outcome is the following procedure for most, and preferably all, projects that have international implications:

(a)   IASC and national standard setters would co-ordinate their work plans so that when IASC starts a project, national standard setters would also add it to their own work plans so that they can play a full part in developing an international consensus.   Similarly, where national standard setters start projects, IASC would consider whether it needs to develop a new Standard or revise its existing Standards;

(b)   IASC and national standard setters would co-ordinate their timetables so that national standard setters would aim to publish their own proposals at the same time as IASC proposals and so that the results from national exposure are available in time for IASC to consider, and vice versa. IASC may need, in certain cases, to slow down its own timetable to some extent so that national standard setters can satisfy their own due process requirements. However, to avoid giving national standard setters a veto in IASC's process, IASC would sometimes need to issue its own proposals without significant delay, even if some national standard setters were not yet ready to issue their own proposals;

(c)   members of the Standards Development Committee would not be required to vote for an IASC treatment in their national standard setters, since each country would remain free to adopt IASC standards with amendments or to adopt other standards. However, the existence of an international consensus is clearly one factor that members of national standard setters would consider when they decide how to vote on national standards;

(d)   IASC would continue to publish its own Exposure Drafts and other documents for public comment;

(e)   national standard setters would publish their own Exposure Drafts at approximately the same time as IASC Exposure Drafts and would seek specific comments on any significant divergences between the two Exposure Drafts. The Working Party expects that market forces would make such divergences increasingly rare. In some instances, national standard setters may ask for specific comments on issues of particular relevance to their country or include more detailed guidance than is included in an International Accounting Standard; and

(f)   national standard setters would follow their own full due process, which they would, ideally, choose to integrate with IASC's due process. Issues arising would be considered by national standard setters. This integration would avoid unnecessary delays in completing standards and would also minimise the likelihood of unnecessary differences between the various standards that result. In the same way as for Exposure Drafts, the Working Party expects that it will become increasingly rare for national standard setters to adopt standards that differ from International Accounting Standards.

Comment periods

207.   Until 1996, IASC allowed a comment period of up to six months for Exposure Drafts. In 1996, IASC accelerated its work programme for the core standards that must be completed before IOSCO will consider endorsing International Accounting Standards for cross-border capital raising and listing purposes in all global markets. Since 1996, the comment period for Exposure Drafts has been three months and several Exposure Drafts have been issued at short intervals. Some have expressed a concern that a comment period of three months may sometimes be too short for respondents to understand and evaluate proposals in sufficient depth, particularly for those respondents who rely on local translations of IASC proposals.

208.   The acceleration of the work programme in 1996 certainly placed strains on IASC's constituents. However, most constituents accepted this, in the hope that it would lead to IOSCO endorsement. The Working Party believes that there is now a case for

IASC to extend its comment periods, although with modern communications it may no longer necessary to have comment periods as long as six months. A minimum of four months may be appropriate, although particularly complex or controversial issues may warrant longer comment periods.

Charging for Exposure Drafts

209.	Some have argued that IASC deters comments by charging for Exposure Drafts, Issues Papers and similar documents. The Working Party acknowledges that this may be the case. However, the need to encourage comments must be balanced against the general principle that those who benefit from IASC should pay for its work.

Translations

210.	In the past, IASC's policy has been to publish International Accounting Standards (as well as other documents, such as Exposure Drafts) only in English. This policy creates a barrier to the use and understanding of International Accounting Standards, particularly in those countries that adopt the standards through domestic legislation.

211.	The Board has sometimes given authority to the Members of IASC and others to prepare translations of the approved text of exposure drafts and International Accounting Standards. International Accounting Standards have been translated into more than 30 languages.

212.	There have been criticisms of some existing translations of International Accounting Standards. Although IASC has no responsibility for these translations, these criticisms may reflect adversely on IASC. More importantly, lack of quality in translations may lead to divergent or even unacceptable interpretations of IASC's standards. The Working Party believes that IASC should explore ways of establishing quality control of these translations, possibly by working with local standard setters and accountancy bodies.

213.	IASC has recently published German and Russian translations of its standards. These are the first translations that IASC has undertaken. IASC aims to publish further translations and has already started work on a Polish translation. The objective of such translations is to:

(a)	promote the use of International Accounting Standards;

(b)	ensure that users of International Accounting Standards have access to high quality translations; and

(c)	raise revenue.

214.	The Working Party recommends that IASC should publish translations of its standards in other languages, preferably on a self-financing basis. For certain languages, a translation of International Accounting Standards may not generate sufficient revenue to cover the cost. It may be possible to obtain funding for these translations from national and international development agencies and similar bodies.

6.   IMPLEMENTATION, ENFORCEMENT AND TRAINING

215.   IASC's work does not end with the publication of standards. IASC must also work in partnership with national standard setters and regulators and encourage them to adopt requirements that are consistent with International Accounting Standards. The Working Party believes that it is not the role of IASC to review national standards in order to assess actively whether those national standards result in compliance with International Accounting Standards.

216.   Some argue that IASC should be more pro-active in identifying departures by preparers from International Accounting Standards (or from national requirements that are consistent with International Accounting Standards) and reporting those departures to national enforcement agencies, IOSCO and the professional accountancy bodies that are members of IFAC and IASC. In principle, the Working Party believes that it would be desirable for IASC to play a more pro-active role in this area. However, the Working Party recognises that IASC does not have the resources to do this effectively. Also, IASC lacks both legal authority to take action and legal protection from those who dispute alleged departures.   In the Working Party's view, identifying and dealing with such departures is primarily a matter for auditors, professional accountancy bodies, IFAC, national enforcement agencies and supranational bodies such as IOSCO and the Basle Committee.

217.   The Working Party believes that IASC should give advice to national regulators and other enforcement agencies in their efforts to enforce national standards that comply with International Accounting Standards, but only if the agency in question both:

(a)   pays for the advice on a fully self-financing basis; and

(b)   gives IASC satisfactory indemnities against legal action by those who dispute alleged departures.

218.   IFAC's draft strategic plan proposes that IFAC should:

(a)   propose a policy and procedures for reviewing the commitments of member bodies in meeting IFAC and IASC standards and guidelines and for ensuring that member bodies have appropriate arrangements for monitoring the observance by their members of such standards and guidelines; and

(b)   publish the first results of a review of the extent to which member bodies meet their commitments and of the appropriateness of their monitoring procedures.

IFAC's education committee may also have a role.

219.   Some national standard setters publish training material, illustrative examples and other implementation guidance, such as staff bulletins. However, IASC has published such material only on an experimental basis, because of lack of human resources. Similarly, IASC does not generally give training courses and does not provide a technical enquiry service. This is because of concerns that such material, although not officially authoritative, might be perceived to have quasi-authoritative status - and so might appear to undermine IASC's due process. Nevertheless, such material would undoubtedly meet a need and it may also be a useful source of revenue.

220. The Working Party believes that IASC should consider publishing training material, illustrative examples and other implementation guidance, such as staff bulletins and, perhaps, also giving training courses. However, at this stage IASC should not provide a technical enquiry service.

7. FUNDING

IASC'S CURRENT FUNDING

221. IASC's current income and expenditure is summarised in appendix 4.

222. Currently, a charge is made to Board Members to cover the budgeted excess of expenditure over other income. The same amount is charged to all Board members, except that the Council of IFAC may decide to reimburse wholly or in part the share charged to one or more Board Members. IFAC currently reimburses the cost of one Board seat and this subsidy is shared equally by India, Sri Lanka and Zimbabwe. In addition, IFAC contributes one ninth of the total amount charged to Board Members.

223. IASC direct costs are remarkably low, largely because many volunteers give their time free, and because IASC relies heavily on research already carried out by national standard setters. Also, some organisations and individuals do not charge their full travel and other costs to IASC. In addition, joint projects with national standard setters sometimes involve staff support by those national standard setters at no cost to IASC (other than direct travel costs).

224. IASC reimburses:

(a) the travelling, hotel and incidental expenses of attendance at Board meetings by one Board Representative from each Board Member;

(b) the Chairman for expenses incurred in attending Board meetings and otherwise on behalf of IASC; and

(c) the travelling, hotel and incidental expenses of members of Steering Committees, the Advisory Council and the Executive Committee.

225. IASC does not take out insurance cover for members of the Board or Steering Committees.

FUNDING IASC FOR THE FUTURE

226. The current method of funding IASC is open to a number of criticisms:

(a) although international travel and the need to research issues in an international context suggest a need for substantial resources, IASC's resources are remarkably modest. This leads to disproportionate demands on the time of Board Representatives, Technical Advisors and the staff;

(b) there is a conflict between the promotion of IAS (especially in poorer countries) and the need to raise funds ("the user pays"). For example, IASC's policy of charging for Exposure Drafts may deter comments;

(c) existing sources of revenue could be threatened by increased use of the Internet and by the increasing availability of national standards that are identical to, or very closely based on, International Accounting Standards;

(d) donations may undermine IASC's actual or perceived independence;

(e)   there is a lack of geographical balance in corporate donations. As a result, it may appear that IASC gives more weight to the views of countries that provide a higher level of donations;

(f)   IASC relies on volatile and uncertain sources of funding. This inhibits long-term planning, diverts scarce staff time and makes it difficult to recruit permanent staff;

(g)   the direct and indirect cost of Board seats deters developing and emerging countries from applying to join the Board;

(h)   the limitations of IASC's resources have forced it to prioritise projects aimed primarily at the needs of developed capital markets and to pay less attention to identifying and meeting any specific needs of developing countries and of countries in East and Central Europe and in Asia that are in transition from centrally planned economies to market driven economies; and

(i)   many organisations (including accountancy bodies that are not on the Board, stock exchanges, governments and national standard setters and others) benefit from IASC's work but do not provide funding. Also, the fact that IASC's only members are professional accountancy bodies is an impediment to fund-raising in some countries.

227.   National standard setters are funded in a variety of ways, for example:

(a)   the Australian Accounting Standards Board raises half its operating costs from government contribution, one third from the two accounting bodies and the balance from sale of publications. A special surcharge on stock exchange filing fees has been agreed for a two-year term, to help fund a programme to harmonise Australian standards with International Accounting Standards;

(b)   Canada's Accounting Standards Board is funded entirely by the Canadian Institute of Chartered Accountants (CICA), through membership fees and sales of courses and publications, although the CICA's Task Force on Standard Setting recently recommended that external funding sources should be pursued, with the goal of achieving a more broadly-financed accounting standards function;

(c)   the UK's Accounting Standards Board raises about 85% of its operating costs in roughly equal contributions from national government, the business community (through a combination of stock exchange listing fees and funding from the Bank of England on behalf of the banking sector and a variety of other financial institutions) and the accounting profession. The balance of its budget comes from sale of publications; and

(d)   the USA's Financial Accounting Standards Board raises two thirds of its operating costs from the sale of publications and the balance is raised by the Financial Accounting Foundation through contributions by accounting firms, industry, banks and investment firms.

228.   The level of funding needed by IASC, and the appropriate balance between different sources of funding, will depend on the nature of any changes made to IASC's structure and activities.

229. Preferably, IASC would need to increase its annual funding from approximately £2 million to around £5 million at current prices to implement the possible revised structure and due process described in paragraphs 124-214 (see appendix 4 for a breakdown). This amount excludes costs that, under the Working Party's proposals, would be borne by national standard setters and others. These costs would amount to between, perhaps, £1 million and £1.5 million. The amount of £5 million also excludes time costs for volunteers.

230. The Working Party believes that IASC needs more secure funding based on a formula, not a constant money drive, so as not to divert Trustee and staff time. There may be a need to use different formulas in different countries. There are several different ways of raising national contributions:

     (a) directly from Board members (including perhaps observers) and/or Members of IASC;

     (b) from a variety of groups in each country who benefit from IASC's work (e.g. preparers, users, regulators, the accountancy profession); or

     (c) indirectly from groups who benefit from IASC's work, with Trustees and/or Members of IASC in each country taking responsibility for collecting the contributions for their countries. For example, it may be desirable to have some degree of commitment to funding over some minimum period, perhaps through organisations in each larger country, to facilitate longer-term planning.

231. The Working Party supports the general principle that those who benefit from IASC's work should pay for its work. The beneficiaries include users of financial statements, business enterprises, auditors, the accountancy profession in general, stock exchanges, regulators, central banks, governments and other government and intergovernmental agencies. However, it is not easy to identify all of those who benefit from IASC's work or to devise a fair way of sharing the cost between the different groups of beneficiaries. The Working Party would welcome suggestions on this.

232. In looking at various funding models, the Working Party considered a number of points, including the following:

     (a) the enterprises that gain the greatest financial benefit from IASC's work are listed enterprises. Therefore, stock exchanges should be an important source of funding. It would seem equitable that all stock exchanges should contribute on a collective basis to remove the incentive for some stock exchanges to be "free riders" – benefiting from IASC's work without paying for it;

     (b) Trustees or member bodies could, perhaps, act as agents for fund-raising in their own countries/constituencies, working to targets agreed to be fair;

     (c) representation of a broad range of constituencies on the Standards Development Committee, Board and Foundation should help fund-raising, as constituents will be more willing to fund a process in which they have representation;

     (d) IASC may be able to persuade enterprises to endow IASC with permanent capital, as a source of investment income to fund part or all of IASC's work;

(e)   without a fair and equitable agreement for sharing publications revenue, publications revenue might drop if national standard setters adopted IAS and companies looked to national requirements instead of to IASC pronouncements;

(f)   by co-operating on projects on a rotational basis, national standard setters may save substantial costs overall. Therefore, it would be reasonable for national standard setters to devote significant resources to the Standards Development Committee (salary of the individual serving on the Standards Development Committee, travel costs, staff support, space, communications);

(g)   professional accountancy bodies carry out the standard setting role in many countries. Some of them may be reluctant to finance an international body when the majority of their local members do not operate in the international arena, as those local members may not realise how international co-operation leverages the resources that are available for standard-setting. However, they may be able to contribute funding not only in cash but also through secondments and through outsourcing of work to them; and

(h)   developing countries are unlikely to have the resources to pay a full contribution towards the cost of IASC. However, although any contribution structure is likely to include a subsidy from more established economies, this is likely to be in the public interest and in the interests of both developing and more established economies. Bodies such as the United Nations and the International Finance Corporation may be willing to support translations of International Accounting Standards and other work by IASC for emerging markets. They may also be willing to fund part of the cost of a Board seat for developing countries, as IFAC does at present.

233.   The Working Party sees merit in a funding model that relies more or less equally on funding from a number of reasonably well-defined groups. An example would be a model that looks to the accountancy profession, government and the business and financial community to provide roughly equal proportions of IASC's funding. The most effective and efficient way to collect the business community's contribution might be through stock exchanges. The Working Party recognises that funding is a vital issue and aims to develop a more detailed funding plan during the period for public comment on this Discussion Paper. In the meantime, the Working Party would welcome comments on funding.

234.   IASC will need continued help with fund-raising from the Advisory Council until any new structure can be put in place.

235.   The Working Party proposes that the Standards Development Advisory Committee should be run on a self-financing basis.

8. CONCLUSION

236. The completion of IASC's current work programme to develop the IOSCO core standards is now imminent. However, IASC will face even greater challenges as it works, in partnership with national standard setters, for further convergence of national accounting standards and practices with high-quality global accounting standards. Therefore, it is vital to give IASC the right structure for the beginning of the twenty-first century. The Working Party invites all parties affected by accounting standards to play a full part in this important debate.

Appendix 1

IASC Constitution

(approved by the Members of IASC on 11th October 1992)

Definitions

The following terms are used in this Constitution with the meanings specified:

Members of IASC shall be the Members defined in clause 3.

Board Members shall be the countries and organisations defined in clause 4. Board Members need not be Members of IASC.

Board Representatives shall be the individuals appointed to represent the Board Members in accordance with clause 6.

Country shall include two or more countries that may be appointed jointly as a Board Member.

Name and Objectives

1. The name of the organisation shall be the International Accounting Standards Committee (IASC).

2. The objectives of IASC are:

   (a) to formulate and publish in the public interest accounting standards to be observed in the presentation of financial statements and to promote their worldwide acceptance and observance; and

   (b) to work generally for the improvement and harmonisation of regulations, accounting standards and procedures relating to the presentation of financial statements.

Membership

3. The Members of the International Accounting Standards Committee shall consist of all professional accountancy bodies that are members of the International Federation of Accountants (IFAC).

The Board

4. The business of IASC shall be conducted by a Board consisting of:

   (a) up to thirteen countries as nominated and appointed by the Council of IFAC that shall be represented by Members of IASC, and

   (b) up to four organisations having an interest in financial reporting co-opted under clause 12(a).

5. (a) The term of appointment of a Board Member selected under clause 4(a) shall be no more than five years. A retiring Board Member shall be eligible for re-appointment.

   (b) The term of appointment of a Board Member co-opted under clause 4(b) shall be determined by the Board at the time of appointment.

6. The Board Members may nominate not more than two Board Representatives from their country or organisation to serve on the Board. The Board Representatives from each country or organisation may be accompanied at meetings of the Board by a Technical Adviser.

7. The Board Representatives and the persons nominated to carry out particular assignments or to join steering committees/working parties/groups shall not regard themselves as representing sectional interests but shall be guided by the need to act in the public interest.

8. The President of IFAC, or his designate, accompanied by not more than one technical adviser, shall be entitled to attend meetings of the Board of IASC, be entitled to the privilege of the floor, but shall not be entitled to vote.

9. The Board shall prepare a report on its work each year and send it to the Members of IASC, the Council of IFAC, and other interested individuals and organisations.

Chairman

10. The Board shall be presided over by a Chairman elected for a term of two-and-a-half years by the Board Representatives from among their number. The Chairman shall not be eligible for re-election. The Board Member providing the Chairman shall be entitled to a further Board Representative.

Voting at Board Meetings

11. Each Board Member shall have one vote which may be taken by a show of hands or by written ballot. Except where otherwise provided either in this Constitution or in the operating procedures, decisions shall be taken on a simple majority of the Board.

Responsibilities and Powers

12. The Board shall have the power to:

   (a) invite up to four organisations having an interest in financial reporting to be co-opted on to the Board;

   (b) remove from membership of the Board any Board Member whose financial contribution determined under clause 14(d) is more than one year in arrears or which fails to be represented at two successive Board meetings;

   (c) publish documents relating to international accounting issues for discussion and comment provided a majority of the Board votes in favour of publication;

   (d) issue documents in the form of exposure drafts for comment (including amendments to existing Standards) in the name of the International Accounting Standards Committee provided at least two-thirds of the Board votes in favour of publication;

(e) issue International Accounting Standards provided that at least three-quarters of the Board votes in favour of publication;

(f) establish operating procedures so long as they are not inconsistent with the provisions of this Constitution;

(g) enter into discussions, negotiations or associations with outside bodies and generally promote the worldwide improvement and harmonisation of accounting standards;

(h) seek and obtain funds from Members of IASC and non-members which are interested in supporting the objectives of IASC provided that such funding is organised in such a way that it does not impair the independence, or the appearance of independence, of IASC.

Issue of Discussion Documents, Exposure Drafts and International Accounting Standards

13. (a) Discussion documents and exposure drafts shall be distributed by the Board to all Members of IASC. A suitable period shall be allowed for respondents to submit comments.

(b) Dissentient opinions will not be included in any exposure drafts or International Accounting Standards promulgated by the Board.

(c) Exposure drafts and International Accounting Standards may be distributed to such governments, standard-setting bodies, stock exchanges, regulatory and other agencies and individuals as the Board may determine.

(d) The approved text of any exposure draft or International Accounting Standard shall be that published by IASC in the English language. The Board may give authority to the Members of IASC and others to prepare translations of the approved text and to publish the approved text of exposure drafts and International Accounting Standards.

Financial Arrangements

14. (a) An annual budget for the ensuing calendar year shall be prepared by the Board each year and sent to the Board Members and to the Council of IFAC.

(b) The Board shall determine the aggregate amount of the net budgeted expenditure which should be borne by the Board Members and by IFAC.

(c) IFAC shall contribute 5% of the aggregate amount determined under (b) in January and 5% in July of each year. The remainder of the aggregate amount determined under (b) shall be borne by the Board Members, except that the Council of IFAC may decide to reimburse wholly or in part the share charged to one or more Board Members.

(d) The Board Members shall contribute on 1st January and 1st July each year a sum in such proportions as shall be decided by a three-quarters vote of the Board. Unless otherwise agreed, Board Members shall contribute equally to the annual budget. Board Members which are represented on the Board for part only of a calendar year shall contribute a pro rata proportion calculated by reference to the period of their representation on the Board in that year.

(e) The Committee shall reimburse the travelling, hotel and incidental expenses of attendance at Board meetings by one Board Representative from each Board Member.

In addition, the Committee shall reimburse the Chairman for expenses incurred in attending Board meetings and otherwise on behalf of IASC.

(f) The Board shall determine in its operating procedures what other expenses shall be a charge against the income of the Committee.

(g) The Board shall annually prepare financial statements and submit them for audit and send copies thereof to the Members of IASC and to the Council of IFAC.

Board Meetings

15. Meetings of the Board shall be held at such times and in such places as the Board Members may mutually agree.

Meetings of the Members of IASC

16. A meeting of the Members of IASC shall be held in conjunction with each General Assembly of IFAC.

17. Each Member of IASC shall have one vote. The method of voting shall be determined by the meeting and shall be either by a show of hands or by ballot. A Member of IASC may give a proxy to another Member of IASC to vote on its behalf subject to the Chairman receiving notice from the Member of IASC giving the proxy prior to the meeting.

Administrative Office

18. The location of the administrative office of the Committee shall be determined by the Board.

Amendments to Constitution

19. Amendments to this Constitution shall be discussed with the Council of IFAC and shall require a three-quarters majority of the Board and approval by the Members of IASC as expressed by a simple majority of those voting.

This revised Constitution was approved by the Members of IASC at a meeting in Washington D.C., United States of America on 11th October 1992.

Appendix 2

Strategy Working Party - Membership and Terms of Reference

The Strategy Working Party was appointed by the Chairman and Deputy Chairman of IASC, in accordance with authority delegated by the IASC Board. Its members are:

Edward Waitzer (Chairman)	*Partner, Stikeman, Elliott* *Former Chairman, Ontario Securities Commission* *Former Chairman, IOSCO Technical Committee*	*Canada*
Georges Barthès de Ruyter	*Chairman, Conseil National de la Comptabilité* *Former Chairman of IASC*	*France*
Jacques Manardo	*Chairman - Europe, Deloitte Touche Tohmatsu International*	*France*
Werner Seifert	*Chief Executive Officer, Deutsche Börse AG*	*Germany*
Kazuo Hiramatsu	*Professor of Accounting, Kwansei Gakuin University* *Member, Business Accounting Deliberation Council*	*Japan*
Peter Sjöstrand	*Partner, BZ Group (Switzerland)* *Board member, Pharma Vision*	*Sweden*
Sir David Tweedie	*Chairman, Accounting Standards Board*	*United Kingdom*
Anthony Cope	*Board member, Financial Accounting Standards Board*	*USA*
David Ruder	*Professor of Law, Northwestern University* *Trustee, Financial Accounting Foundation* *Former Chairman, US Securities and Exchange Commission*	*USA*
Birgitta Kantola	*Vice President, Finance and Planning, International Finance Corporation*	
Frank Harding	*President, International Federation of Accountants*	
Stig Enevoldsen	*Chairman, IASC*	
Michael Sharpe	*Past Chairman, IASC*	
Sir Bryan Carsberg	*Secretary-General, IASC*	

The Board gave the Strategy Working Party the following terms of reference:

The Strategy Working Party should review the strategy of IASC generally for the period following completion of the current work programme in 1998.

Without limit to the generality of the foregoing, the working party should consider whether a major focus of the work of IASC after 1998 should be to narrow further the differences between national standards and international standards. It should consider what procedures would be appropriate for this task and, in particular, whether some new form of association, agreement or working arrangement between IASC and national standard setters is desirable.

The working party should consider whether any other new focus should be incorporated in the IASC work plan.

The working party should consider the procedures adopted by IASC and form a view as to whether changes in procedures are needed to reconcile the conflicting requirements of efficient decision-making in a group which has already become very large for the purposes of technical discussions and the requirements of being a highly representative body in which more and more nations have strong claims to be included. Without limitations on the generality of its terms of reference, the working party should consider whether a bicameral approach is desirable (e.g. a small standing committee to prepare proposed standards and a larger group to vote upon their acceptability), whether one or more full-time Board Members are needed and whether meetings of the Board or its committees should be open to the public.

The working party should consider what role IASC should take in educational and training activities relating to its standards.

The working party should review arrangements for funding IASC taking account of the success of the fund-raising programme over the last two years and the needs implied by the proposed strategy for IASC.

Appendix 3

Foundation Working Party (1994) - summary of recommendations

In 1992, the IASC Board set up a Foundation Working Party to review the structure and organisation of IASC. In 1994, the Foundation Working Party recommended to the Board that:

(a)   IASC should create a high level, international Advisory Council consisting of outstanding individuals in senior positions from the accountancy profession, the business community, other users of financial statements and other backgrounds. The objectives of the Council should be to promote the acceptability of International Accounting Standards, enhance the credibility of the work of IASC and ensure that the necessary level of funding is available for IASC's work;

(b)   the Board should continue to deal with all technical issues associated with the work of IASC. It should continue to work for the improvement and harmonisation of financial reporting through the development of International Accounting Standards and the promotion of their use in published financial statements;

(c)   the Board should include a proper balance of representatives from public accounting, the business community and the other users of financial statements as well as representatives who are directly involved in the work of the national standard setters; and

(d)   the Board should work directly with other standard setters in order to achieve common improvements in accounting standards as well as greater compatibility between national requirements and International Accounting Standards and between the national requirements of different countries.

The Foundation Working Party believed that these recommendations could be implemented within the existing IASC Constitution and in such a way that allows IASC the flexibility to adapt further as circumstances demand.

However, the Foundation Working Party also indicated that its recommendations did not preclude further evolution if such evolution were necessary to increase the acceptability of International Accounting Standards and increase the resources available to IASC. The Working Party considered some aspects of the form that such further evolution could take, in particular the replacement of the Advisory Council by a Foundation which would have certain powers and responsibilities assigned by a revised IASC Constitution, rather than delegated to it by the Board.

Appendix 4

Summary of IASC's Income and Expenditure

The following table summarises IASC's income and expenditure for 1997, in £'000, and the possible cost, in today's prices, of the revised structure set out in paragraphs 125-200.

	1997	Revised structure
Operating revenue		
Contributions from Board/Board Members and IFAC	725	1,000
Other contributions	742	742
New funding needed to break even	**0**	**2,198**
World Bank contribution for Agriculture Project	56	0
	1,523	3,940
Publications revenue	952	1,330
Less direct costs of publications sales	(364)	(420)
	588	910
Total operating revenue	**2,111**	**4,850**
Project expenses		
Standards Development Committee salaries (excluding those borne nationally)	0	800
Staff costs	827	1,400
Steering Committee / task force meetings	241	300
Board / Board meetings	274	650
Board and Trustees' Chairmen's salaries (2 @50%)	0	200
Trustees' travel	0	125
SIC Meetings	60	125
Other meetings	158	200
Other operating expenses	61	350
Total project expenses	**1,621**	**4,150**
Support expenses		
Staff costs	140	250
Occupancy and equipment expenses	161	350
Depreciation	32	100
Other operating expenses	57	150
Total support expenses	**390**	**850**
Total operating expenses	**2,011**	**5,000**
Operating revenue more than expenses	**100**	**(150)**
Investment income (net of tax)	86	150
Total revenue less total expenses	**186**	**0**

Appendix 5

Economic Data

Gross Domestic Product

		US$ billion
1	USA	7,100
2	Japan	4,964
3	Germany	2,252
4	France	1,451
5	UK	1,095
6	Italy	1,088
7	China (including Hong Kong - 142)	887
8	Scandinavia (Denmark, Finland, Norway, Sweden)	607
9	Brazil	580
10	Canada	574
11	Spain	532
12	South Korea	435
13	Netherlands	371
14	Australia	338
15	Russia	332
16	India	320
17	Mexico	305
18	Switzerland	286
19	Argentina	278
20	Taiwan	260
	World total	27,657

Source: The Economist, Pocket World in Figures, 1998

Market Capitalisation

1	USA	6,858
2	Japan	3,667
3	UK	1,407
4	Germany	577
5	France	522
6	Switzerland	434
7	Canada	366
8	Netherlands	356
9	China (including Hong Kong - 304)	346
10	Scandinavia (Denmark, Finland, Norway, Sweden)	323
11	South Africa	281
12	Australia	245
13	Malaysia	223
14	Italy	210
15	Spain	198
16	Taiwan	187
17	South Korea	182
18	Singapore	148
19	Brazil	148
20	Thailand	142

Source: The Economist, Pocket World in Figures, 1998

Largest Exporters as a Percentage of World Trade (Visible and Invisible)

		% of total world exports	Cumulative
1	USA	13.47	13.47
2	Germany	9.82	23.29
3	Japan	9.55	32.84
4	France	6.92	39.76
5	UK	6.37	46.13
6	Italy	4.59	50.72
7	Scandinavia (Denmark, Finland, Norway, Sweden)	4.32	55.04
8	Belgium/Luxembourg	4.24	59.28
9	Netherlands	3.49	62.77
10	Canada	3.11	65.88
11	China (including Hong Kong 0.93)	3.05	68.93
12	Switzerland	2.15	71.08
13	South Korea	2.11	73.19
14	Spain	2.03	75.22
15	Taiwan	1.87	77.09
16	Singapore	1.53	78.62
17	Austria	1.48	80.10
18	Russia	1.36	81.46
19	Mexico	1.30	82.76
20	Malaysia	1.15	83.91

Source: The Economist, Pocket World in Figures, 1998

OECD Member Countries

Australia	Korea
Austria	Luxembourg
Belgium	Mexico
Canada	The Netherlands
Czech Republic	New Zealand
Denmark	Norway
Finland	Poland
France	Portugal
Germany	Spain
Greece	Sweden
Hungary	Switzerland
Iceland	Turkey
Ireland	UK
Italy	USA
Japan	

Appendix 6

Possible Timetable for Implementing the Working Party's Proposals

Deadline for comments on this Discussion Paper	30 April 1999
Working Party to discuss comments received	May 1999
Working Party to meet IASC Board to discuss the comment letters	July 1999
Nominating Committee (current Advisory Council plus recent past Chairmen of IASC and IFAC) and IFAC, IAFEI, ICCFAA, FIBV, IAAER to begin work on identifying candidates to be the first Trustees	July 1999
Working Party to finalise proposals	September 1999
Council of IFAC to discuss constitutional changes	November 1999
IASC Board to discuss constitutional changes	November 1999
Nominating Committee (current Advisory Council plus recent past Chairmen of IASC and IFAC) to appoint the first six 'at large' Trustees and to consider the six 'constituency' trustees by nominated by IFAC and bodies such as IAFEI, ICCFAA, FIBV, IAAER and to appoint one of the Trustees to be the first Chairman of the Trustees *[These appointments will be provisional, pending approval of the constitutional changes]*	December 1999
First meetings of provisional Trustees and Selection Sub-Committee, to begin selection process for Standards Development Committee and enlarged Board	January 2000
IASC Board to approve constitutional changes, subject to approval by Members of IASC	March 2000
Meeting of IASC Members to approve constitutional changes	May 2000
Trustees to appoint Standards Development Committee and enlarged Board	June 2000
Enlarged Board and SDC come into effect	1 July 2000
Trustees to appoint / reappoint Technical Director and Commercial Director	3rd Quarter 2000